1

Devotional

THE WAY OF MIRACLES

Forty days walking with Jesus

VitalCenter.org

Translated from "O Caminho de Milagres" by Vital Jr.
Based on the João Ferreira de Almeida version, 1819
Copyright © 2025 by Vital Foundation
United States of America

ISBN: 979-8-9863817-7-0
Paperback version

First Edition

Visit our website
VitalCenter.org
Contact
Vital@usa.com

Dedication

I dedicate this work with deep gratitude to Pastor Vital Barreto Pereira—a man who devoted his life to the cause of the Gospel—and to the beloved Professor Ilseny Figueiredo Pereira. It was they who planted in my heart, from an early age, an unconditional love for Christ Jesus. Every page of this book carries the fruit of their teachings and example. Without their sacred influence, none of these words would exist.

Vital Jr.

PREFACE

For forty days, I walked through the desert, and forty times I resisted temptation. Each day dragged on like a year, each night seemed endless. Why such solitude? How much easier it would be if my family were with me, if my friends kept me company... One day, I will tell of the wild beasts that watched me from a distance, seeing me as prey, of the moon and stars that lit my path. Everything in life begins with sacrifice, a trial, a long road to travel. If I persevere in faith, I will reach the destination I have chosen. Is this the destiny prepared for me? It does not matter. If I believe, I will attain what I have dreamed of.

I endured forty days of hunger and pain, and for each of them, I performed a miracle that transformed lives—sometimes of one, sometimes of many, and at certain moments, of the entire world. Men cried out my name, pleading for mercy; women shed tears of anguish, yet from the children flowed perfect praise. The blind arrived guided and left knowing the way, and the mute, after encountering me, went forth telling stories of joy. Even those who bore chains in their souls found freedom and began singing songs of victory. Many brought me their impossibilities, and I taught them: "Everything is possible for the one who believes."

Many times, death crossed my path, but I renamed it as life, transforming its purpose into the beginning of all things. The world rushed past those who could not move—until they heard my words: "Rise and walk!" To the abandoned, I offered a home. To the sick, I chose to heal.

INTRODUCTION

FORTY DAYS HE FASTED IN THE DESERT.

FORTY NIGHTS HE PRAYED FOR US.

FORTY DAYS HE WAS TEMPTED.

FORTY MIRACLES HE LEFT FOR US.

FORTY DAYS FROM RESURRECTION TO ASCENSION.

If we meditate for forty days on His miracles and wonders, we will learn much about His goodness, mercy, and power. If we compare ourselves to the characters of these miracles, we will certainly find many common points. Not everyone received healing; some received deliverance, others freedom and salvation. However, all received their miracle. If Jesus did it for them, why wouldn't He do it for us as well? If we write our plans and meditate with faith on God's promises, many of our dreams will come true.

At the end of each miracle, you will have the opportunity to reflect, meditate, and write everything God spoke through the ministry of Jesus. Write your requests and prayers, and after a year, return to see the miracles God has worked in your life. For it is impossible to walk with Jesus and not receive something from His goodness and mercy!

INDEX

THE VICTORY OVER TEMPTATION

Love came into the world to save it, and His desire was to be with everyone, but He suffered alone, separated from everything and everyone. This episode occurred right after His baptism. He was led into the Judean desert, an arid and inhospitable region, where He faced a period of solitude and trial.

Then the Holy Spirit led Jesus into the desert to be tempted by the Devil. After forty days and forty nights without eating, Jesus was hungry. The Devil then approached Him and said,
— If you are the Son of God, tell these stones to become bread.
Jesus replied,
— The Scriptures say:
"Man shall not live by bread alone, but by every word that comes from the mouth of God."
Then the Devil took Jesus to Jerusalem, to the Holy City, and placed Him on the highest point of the Temple. He said,
— If you are the Son of God, throw yourself down, for the Scriptures say:
"God will command His angels concerning you, and they will lift you up in their hands, so that you will not strike your foot against a stone."
Jesus replied,
— But the Scriptures also say: "Do not put the Lord your God to the test."
Finally, the Devil took Jesus to a very high mountain, showed Him all the kingdoms of the world and their splendor, and said,
— All this I will give you if you bow down and worship me.
Jesus replied,
— Away from me, Satan! For it is written:
"Worship the Lord your God, and serve Him only."
Then the Devil left Him, and angels came and attended to Him.
(Matthew 4:1-11)

When Satan encountered Jesus, he saw the perfect and immaculate image, just like the first man. Having defeated Adam, he might have thought he could defeat Jesus with the same temptations common to all men. According to 1 John 2:16, the three areas of temptation are related to the "desires of the flesh," "desires of the eyes," and "pride of life." These categories help to understand how Satan tempted Jesus, as described in the episode of the temptations in the desert. Below are the three temptations of Jesus and how they align with these areas mentioned in the letter of John.

Covetousness of the eyes: Satan showed Jesus all the kingdoms of the world and promised Him power and glory if He bowed down and worshiped him. This temptation relates to the covetousness of the eyes, the desire for visible and immediate possessions, such as power and wealth. "Again, the devil took Him to a very high mountain and showed Him all the kingdoms of the world and their glory. And he said to Him, 'All this I will give you if you will fall down and worship me.'" Matthew 4:8-9

Lust of the flesh: When Satan asked Jesus to turn stones into bread, he was appealing to Jesus' physical need, hunger. This aligns with the lust of the flesh, which is the desire to satisfy physical and material needs, often in a selfish or uncontrolled manner. "If you are the Son of God, command that these stones become bread." Matthew 4:3

Pride of life: When Satan asked Jesus to throw Himself down from the pinnacle of the temple to test if God would save Him, he was tempting Him with the pride of life—the temptation to act presumptuously, challenging God and seeking fame or glory through a reckless act. "If you are the Son of God, throw Yourself down from here; for it is written: 'He will command His angels concerning you, to guard you'; and on their hands they will bear you up, lest you strike your foot against a stone.'" Matthew 4:6

10

The only beings capable of overcoming sin were those who had no sin: Adam and Eve. After they sinned in Eden, all of humanity inherited the seed of sin and, for this reason, lost the spiritual level of perfection.

Now, if Adam and Eve, who were sinless, fell into temptation, how could we, born in sin and carrying the seed of sin, overcome temptations on our own? This was an impossibility that Jesus made possible. A being with the seed of sin cannot, by itself, overcome sin. We can only conquer it when we are in Christ, with the mind of Christ, with the Holy Spirit of God, and in the authority of the name of Jesus. Without these weapons, we are easy targets for temptations. No man can claim to overcome sin without the help of Jesus and His Holy Spirit. The Apostle Paul explains this: "I do not do the good I want to do." Romans 7:18-19.

That's why I call everything impossible for man a miracle. Stripped of His glory, alone, and physically weakened by hunger, Jesus was tempted at a very challenging moment. He was tested in everything, but in the end, He prevailed.

It's in these moments that we are most vulnerable: when we are without support, without friends, and without help. Satan knows exactly when to offer us a quick solution to our desires and problems. Jesus performed many miracles, but it was His holiness that qualified Him.

The forty days of fasting of Jesus remind us of the forty years the Hebrew people spent crossing the desert toward the Promised Land. While they failed by giving in to temptations, Jesus demonstrated perfect obedience. With each day Jesus overcame in the desert, it was as if He was restoring the defeat of the people during their forty years of trials. This was the first miracle Jesus performed as a man, a miracle no one else was able to accomplish. For this reason, Jesus came without blemish and perfect to conquer what we could not: overcoming sin.

11

What stood out to you the most?

_____

_____

_____

_____

_____

How can this reflection enhance your spiritual life?

_____

_____

_____

_____

What would you say to Jesus today?

_____

_____

_____

_____

_____

*"No temptation has overtaken you except what is
common to mankind, and God is faithful; He will not let you be
tempted beyond what you can bear. But when you are tempted,
He will also provide a way out so that you can endure it."*
1 Corinthians 10:13

THE WATER INTO WINE

This story took place in Cana of Galilee, probably in the year 30 AD. Although the exact location is still debated, it is believed that Cana was about eight to ten kilometers from Nazareth. It was an agricultural community and, like many Galilean villages, had a strong influence from Jewish culture. At the time, the region was part of the Roman province of Judea. Emperor Tiberius ruled Rome, while Herod Antipas held the position of tetrarch of Galilee. The environment was marked by political and religious tensions, with the Jews frequently at odds with Roman rule. In this atmosphere of instability, the earthly ministry of the Messiah was about to begin.

Weddings were significant social events and involved celebrations that could last between five and seven days. To ensure that everything was in order, a master of ceremonies (or steward of the feast) was appointed, responsible for organizing the celebration and ensuring that everything went smoothly, including the provision of food and wine.

At that time, marriages were arranged by families, and the bride and groom had little say in the matter. Imagine yourself reading a book, just like now, when your guardians call you to announce that they have found your spouse. For a long time, I considered this practice absurd, a true imposition. How could it be? Am I not allowed to choose the person I want to spend the rest of my life with? However, on the other hand, I realized that all the pressure and difficulty of finding the perfect match disappear. Deep down, I would think: "If something goes wrong, it's not my fault at all, and no one can blame me."

I imagine the young man's parents visiting the young woman's family to arrange the marriage, saying they had observed her good behavior and wished for her to be their son's bride. In this culture, parents were responsible for asking the important and relevant questions for married life. At the first meeting of the couple, they would not discuss these matters, as everything had already been arranged by their families. Instead, they would talk about life, about themselves, or perhaps about how beautiful the wedding celebration would be, with all their family and friends gathered to celebrate this unique and unforgettable moment. Their anticipation would only grow as the wedding day approached.

Despite all the preparation for the feast, the bride and groom could never have imagined that an essential element of the celebration might run out. The narration of this story begins in the second chapter of the book of John.

Two days later, there was a wedding in the village of Cana, in the region of Galilee, and the mother of Jesus was present. Jesus and His disciples were also invited to the celebration. When the wine ran out, the mother of Jesus said to Him:
— The wine is gone.
Jesus replied:
— Your concerns are not mine. My time has not yet come.
Then she instructed the servants:
— Do everything He tells you. Nearby, there were six stone jars, each capable of holding between eighty and one hundred twenty liters of water. These jars were used by the Jews in their purification rituals. Jesus said to the servants:
— Fill the jars with water.
And they filled them to the brim. Then Jesus ordered:
— Now draw some out and take it to the master of the banquet.
The servants obeyed, and when the banquet master tasted the water, it had turned into wine. He did not know where the wine had come from, but the servants knew. Then he called the groom and said:
— Everyone serves the good wine first, and after the guests have had plenty to drink, they serve the inferior wine. But you have kept the best wine until now.

This was the first miracle performed by Jesus in Cana of Galilee. In this way, He revealed His divine nature, and His disciples believed in Him. John 2:1-12

While the hosts of the feast were running back and forth, trying to understand and solve the lack of wine, Jesus simply observed and waited for the right moment to perform the miracle. I believe that when Mary approached Jesus for help, it had not yet been determined that the problem had no solution. Mary's presence suggests a close relationship with the host family, perhaps as a relative or friend, but her attempt to help had to wait for the right time for the miracle to happen. Women in the community played an important role in organizing celebrations, including overseeing the preparation of food and drinks.

The presence of wine was essential, symbolizing joy and hospitality. Its absence would have been an unforgettable embarrassment for the host family. Everyone would remember this wedding as the event where the wine ran out, but Jesus' presence changed that story. He turned the feast into a moment marked by a great miracle, where the guest transformed water into provision, lack into abundance, and shame into prosperity.

The bride and groom, facing this problem, must have asked themselves: "What do we do now?" That was the moment Jesus decided to act and commanded the servants to fill the stone jars. Their obedience in following Jesus' instructions was fundamental to the miracle. This shows us that even though the miracle was supernatural, our natural actions may be required. Without the jars, without the water, without the servants, without patience, and without obedience, the miracle might not have happened.

With Jesus in our lives, the question "What now?" never goes unanswered. However, like the bride and groom, we must wait for the right time, learn to obey the Lord's guidance, and believe that the One who can perform all miracles is by our side. Many, like the master of the banquet, will ask us how this miracle happened in our lives. The master of the banquet had no idea what was happening behind the scenes of the celebration; to him, everything happened suddenly and naturally. His surprise was how the best was saved for last.

15

The natural world offers a false sense of freedom and temporary joy in the beginning—everything comes easily—but in the end, we find ourselves facing suffering, sadness, and disappointment. What once seemed like fun now brings bondage and dependence, and its fruits lead to the death of our souls. However, when we follow God's guidance, we find peace and eternal life. Our growth and development are always contrary to what is natural. We go through trials and difficulties that challenge our faith.

The bride and groom and Mary had to wait and believe that Jesus was in control of the situation. Mary demonstrated her faith and patience—she waited, did not complain, and even testified to the servants to do everything Jesus commanded. She believed that Jesus could do something.

When we face a difficulty or impossibility, we often quantify and qualify the problem based on our level of resources or the likelihood of finding a solution. If there is a natural possibility or a human resource capable of solving the problem, then we are not truly facing a miracle.

In the case of the bride and groom, the probability and possibility of obtaining enough wine for the entire celebration at that moment were nonexistent. Something so wonderful had never happened before. When we face our impossibilities, we should not think or say that something has never happened before and therefore is impossible. Perhaps God wants to make us an example, just as He did with the bride and groom of Cana. What has never happened to anyone else may happen in our lives, and we will become living witnesses of God's power. With Jesus' intervention, they not only solved the problem of the feast but also received much more than they needed. The abundance of that precious wine could even have been sold for a good price, bringing additional benefits to the family.

The original writer of this story does not mention the reason for the lack of wine at the feast. Whenever something goes wrong, we are quick to investigate the reason and, above all, to find out who was to blame. We do the same in our lives: when something terrible happens, we immediately seek a cause and someone to blame. Why is my marriage not working? Why are my finances in disarray? Why did this tragedy happen in my life? These are valid and honest questions in most cases.

However, all these questions, even without answers, can be resolved if Jesus is present in the conversation. He has the answers we need; He knows why the wine ran out at the feast. It does not matter why your problems exist—what matters is that, in the end, Jesus performs the miracle. What is in the past remains in the past, and the past does not return. If your hope is in the One who can work miracles, the future awaits you with victory.

The miracle of turning water into wine carries so many spiritual elements that, if we are not careful, we may fail to notice that wine is referred to as a symbol of Jesus' blood, shed for all. Just as everyone at the feast received the wine Jesus provided, those who celebrate the Lord's Supper, using wine as a symbol of His blood, also participate in His redemptive work. From the first miracle to the Last Supper, the message of redemption and the new covenant is powerfully revealed. John 2:1-11

What stood out to you the most?

_____

_____

_____

_____

_____

_____

_____

_____

_____

_____

_____

_____

_____

_____

How can this reflection enhance your spiritual life?

_____

_____

_____

_____

_____

_____

_____

What would you say to Jesus today?

_____

_____

_____

_____

_____

_____

_____

_____

_____

"And my God will supply all your needs according to
His riches in glory in Christ Jesus."
Philippians 4:19

THE OFFICIAL'S SON

A desperate man ran through the city in search of a prophet known for performing miracles. His silent faith was the only thing keeping him moving. Amidst the chaos, he sought a chance, a change. Thus begins the story of the king's official.

Jesus returned to Cana in Galilee, where he had turned water into wine. There was a royal official there who lived in Capernaum. He had a sick son at home. When he heard that Jesus had come from Judea to Galilee, he went to ask him to go to Capernaum and heal his son, who was dying.
Jesus said to the official:
— You only believe when you see great miracles!
He answered:
— Lord, come quickly before my child dies!
— Go back home! Your son will live! — said Jesus.
He believed Jesus' words and left. On the way, he met his servants, who said:
— Your son is alive!
Then he asked what time his son had started to get better. The servants answered:
— Yesterday, at one in the afternoon, the fever left him.
Then the father remembered that it was at that very hour that Jesus had said: "Your son will live." So he and his whole family believed in Jesus. John 4:46-54

Throughout this book, we will observe that Jesus performed miracles in various ways, showing that God's power cannot be limited by our plans or desires. That man left home in search of a miracle. He knew who could perform it and had planned how Jesus would do it. How did he know that Jesus was capable of performing miracles? The city where he lived was the same where the miracle of turning water into wine had occurred.

Perhaps he was among the guests at that wedding. If he was not, he certainly heard about the miracle from those who witnessed it.

Who was this royal official? Was he part of the nobility? He could have been a Jew or someone in an administrative position within the governmental structure of the king. The Bible does not specify his ethnicity or nationality, but it is possible that he was Jewish or had some connection with the local Jewish authority. From the historical context, we know that the king was Herod Antipas, the same one to whom Jesus was taken before being judged by Pilate. Herod asked Jesus to perform a sign because he had heard much about him. Luke 23:8. It is possible that this official later testified to the king about the miracle performed on his son.

The distance between Cana in Galilee and Capernaum is approximately 30 kilometers (about 18 to 20 miles), depending on the exact route. This distance could be covered on foot in about six to eight hours, depending on the conditions and pace of travel. This region was located in the north of Israel, and journeys between these two cities were often made on foot, as was common at the time.

That man could have sent a servant to fetch Jesus, but what he sought was too important to delegate to someone else. When Jesus confronted the faith of those present, he did not give up but insisted, "Lord, come quickly before my child dies!" This could be paraphrased as: "If you go, he will not die!"

There was already faith in his heart, for faith is the certainty of things not seen, and that man had this certainty. Jesus did not need to say, "Have faith!" or "If you believe, you will see the miracle!" He simply declared victory based on that faith, saying, "Go back home! Your son will live!"

Everything he imagined, Jesus did differently. He thought Jesus would go, but he did not. He thought Jesus would pray, lay hands, anoint, but he did none of that. How many times do we try to plan how God should solve our problems? God always has a solution that can surprise us. Imagine if Jesus had said, "I will neither go to your house nor pray for your son!" Could this be why God does not tell us how and when he will perform miracles in our lives?

The official walked the same path twice, but how different those journeys were. On the way there, he walked in haste, desperate and afraid of losing his beloved son. On the way back, he walked with faith in his heart and the certainty of the miracle. Because he believed, the same road revealed two completely different realities. His faith and attitude led him to victory. If he had stayed home lamenting, his son would have died, but he decided to walk even in fear and despair.

Jesus' healing ministry began in a surprising way, beyond human understanding. With just a word, he demonstrated divine power that transcended time and space, performing a miracle from a distance. That word of faith, filled with love, not only healed the official's son but also brought hope and joy, turning pain into a living testimony of Christ's compassion.

That night, amid the celebration of healing, the family experienced the peace and communion that only God's power can provide. Seated at the table, joy and gratitude were palpable, reflecting divine intervention. Meanwhile, in another part of the house, the servants marveled at the miracle, astonished by Jesus' authority. Without a doubt, the question lingered: "How can a man heal with just words?" This question reflected the human struggle to comprehend God's power, something that transcended logic and revealed the true nature of Christ, the Messiah.

This episode not only teaches us about the power of a word spoken in faith but also about the importance of trusting Jesus. The official did not ask for visible signs or great miracles to believe, but he trusted in what Jesus said. His faith was the key to his son's healing.

What stood out to you the most?

_____

_____

_____

_____

_____

How can this reflection enhance your spiritual life?

_____

_____

_____

_____

What would you say to Jesus today?

_____

_____

_____

_____

"The prayer of a righteous person is powerful in its effects. Elijah was a man with a nature like ours, and he prayed earnestly that it would not rain, and for three years and six months, it did not rain on the earth. Then he prayed again, and the sky gave rain, and the earth produced its fruit."

James 5:16b-18

THE MIRACULOUS CATCH

The night before, they had prepared everything for a big fishing trip: the boat, the nets, and the hope. However, they returned only with fatigue, an empty boat, and deep frustration. Thus begins the story of Peter and his fellow fishermen.

One day, Jesus was by the shore of the Sea of Galilee, and the crowd pressed around Him to hear God's message. He saw two boats on the lake, near the shore. The fishermen had left them and were washing their nets. Jesus got into one of the boats, the one belonging to Simon, and asked him to push it out a little from the shore. Then He sat down and began to teach the crowd.
When He had finished speaking, Jesus said to Simon,
— Put out into deep water, and let down the nets for a catch.
Simon answered,
— Master, we worked hard all night and haven't caught anything. But because You say so, I will let down the nets.
When they had done so, they caught such a large number of fish that their nets began to break. So they signaled their partners in the other boat to come and help them, and they came and filled both boats so full that they began to sink.
When Simon Peter saw this, he fell at Jesus' knees and said,
— Go away from me, Lord; I am a sinful man!
For he and all his companions were astonished at the catch of fish they had taken, and so were James and John, the sons of Zebedee, Simon's partners.
Then Jesus said to Simon,
— Don't be afraid; from now on you will fish for people.
So they pulled their boats up on shore, left everything, and followed Him. Luke 5:1-11

After a long night of attempts, the fisherman Peter and his friends decided to return to the shore. I imagine that, in their minds, some questions were bothering them, such as: "What happened today? Why didn't we catch any fish?"

As they were cleaning the nets, there was nothing better to do than think about what had happened. Suddenly, Jesus, who was preaching on the shore, decided to use that boat as a platform for preaching. After a long and frustrating night, Peter could have claimed exhaustion and asked Jesus to use another boat. That would have been a valid excuse, but something inside Peter stirred the desire to help, or perhaps curiosity about Jesus' preaching.

When Jesus told Peter to fish, he responded that they had already fished all night. However, he added that, because of Jesus' command, they would try again. As if by a miracle or pure obedience, Peter discovered the secret to success: obeying Jesus. When he encountered the miracle, he fell to the ground as a sign of reverence and worship. His feeling of incapacity and amazement in the face of Jesus' miraculous power was what he needed to follow Him fully.

The men who had set out to conquer the lake were conquered by a cause greater than they could have ever imagined. Realizing the greatness of Jesus, they left behind the fish, the miracle, and the boat, and began to follow the One who performed the miracles.

The most important part of this miracle was not the fish falling into the net, but the revelation these men had—something they didn't fully understand, yet didn't dare let pass. Now, they were no longer fisherman Peter and his friends, but Jesus' disciples on a mission.

What stood out to you the most?

_____

_____

_____

_____

_____

How can this reflection enhance your spiritual life?

_____

_____

_____

_____

_____

What would you say to Jesus today?

_____

_____

_____

_____

_____

""God cannot lie when He makes a promise and cannot lie when He makes an oath. These things encourage us who seek security in God."
Hebrews 6:18

THE DEMON-POSSESSED IN CAPERNAUM

Before arriving in Capernaum, Jesus was in the region of Galilee, beginning His public ministry. During His visit to the synagogue in Nazareth, the Jews tried to throw Him off a cliff. Now, in Capernaum, we see that wherever Jesus went, something extraordinary happened. Mark begins his narration by highlighting this transformative power.

Jesus and the disciples arrived in the city of Capernaum, and on the Sabbath, He went to teach in the synagogue. The people who listened to Him were amazed at His way of teaching, for Jesus taught with His own authority and not like the teachers of the Law. Then a man possessed by an evil spirit came in and shouted:
— What do you want with us, Jesus of Nazareth? Have you come to destroy us? I know very well who you are: the Holy One sent by God!
Then Jesus commanded the evil spirit:
— Be quiet and come out of him!
The spirit then violently shook the man, let out a loud scream, and left him.
Everyone was astonished and said to one another:
— What does this mean? It is a new teaching given with authority. He even commands evil spirits, and they obey Him.
And Jesus' fame quickly spread throughout the region of Galilee.
Mark 1:21-28

Jesus did not come to earth to break taboos but to save humanity from eternal condemnation. However, in the process, many taboos were broken, and one of them was the belief that evil spirits could not be cast out. During His visit to the synagogue in Nazareth, Jesus declared that He came to bring freedom to the

26

captives and the brokenhearted. Luke 4:18. Wasn't that exactly what He did for this possessed man?

Under the astonished gaze of everyone, He commanded the spirit to leave that poor man. When we see a person in such a state, we may feel fear or contempt, but Jesus looked at him with compassion because that man was enslaved and destroyed by this evil spirit. If Jesus had not visited that synagogue that day, surely this man would have been expelled from the gathering. Yet Jesus did not cast out the man; He cast out the spirit that tormented him.

Throughout His ministry, we will see that, on many occasions, the Jews questioned Jesus about who He really was. However, that spirit immediately and publicly declared in a loud voice that it knew exactly who Jesus was: the Holy One sent by God. Jesus did not need to introduce Himself to that man or preach a sermon for His true identity to be revealed. The light of Jesus was evident in His life. While the religious leaders did not recognize it, the one who walked in darkness could not resist His brightness and authority.

In one of His parables in Mark 4:21, Jesus explains that light cannot be hidden. If we are in Christ, His light will shine in our lives, and the world around us will be impacted. "I know very well who you are!" said that man. This should be the testimony of those who encounter us.

That day marked the beginning of a new life for that man. I believe that as he left that gathering, even those who saw him passing by could notice the difference in his life. I imagine that when he arrived home, people asked, "What happened to you? You were restless and unstable; you couldn't say anything that made sense." Then, perhaps he replied, "I don't know what happened, but I know that I met a man who changed my life. He did not despise me or fear my condition, but He spoke words that set me free from my state of bondage."

What stood out to you the most?

_____

_____

_____

_____

_____

How can this reflection enhance your spiritual life?

_____

_____

_____

_____

What would you say to Jesus today?

_____

_____

_____

_____

_____

"Jesus spoke to them again, saying: I am the light of the world; whoever follows me will not walk in darkness but will have the light of life."

John 8:12

PETER'S MOTHER-IN-LAW

This miracle became known as "The Healing of Peter's Mother-in-Law," but it could also be called "The Night of Miracles." This is how Matthew narrates it:

Jesus went to Peter's house and saw his mother-in-law in bed with a fever. Jesus touched her hand, and the fever left her. Then she got up and began to serve them.

After sunset, the people brought to Jesus many who were possessed by demons. And with just a word, he cast out the evil spirits and healed all who were sick. Jesus did this to fulfill what the prophet Isaiah had said:

"He took our illnesses and bore our diseases." Matthew 8:14

This happened after his visit to the synagogue in Capernaum. Jesus decided to rest at Peter's house, which was also in the same city. After healing Peter's mother-in-law and being served by her, people began arriving after nightfall in search of healing or deliverance.

If we look at the previous miracle in Mark 1:21, we will notice that this took place on a Sabbath. That was why people only went to Peter's house after the Sabbath rest had ended. The law prohibited them from traveling long distances on that day. Even though Jesus' miracles had already spread throughout the city and the possessed man in the Capernaum synagogue had been freed, everyone waited until sunset, which they considered the official end of the Sabbath.

I imagine people standing by their windows anxiously waiting for the Sabbath to end or sitting in their courtyards looking at the sky, longing for the day to be over. The hope of those people was that the end of the day would also mark the end of their troubles.

The streets of Capernaum must have been dark, but many people, carrying their lanterns and lamps, brought their sick and their requests. Those who had not yet heard of the Prophet who healed and delivered the oppressed asked others what was happening and where they were going. Now, many curious people also followed the crowd to Peter's house. These people walking in darkness needed a light to guide them, but they did not yet know that Jesus was the light of the world and the true way.

When they arrived at Peter's house and found Jesus, He healed and delivered all who needed help. I believe that night was filled with miracles, as those who were healed went through the city telling their neighbors what had happened. Suddenly, more and more people came to see the Prophet.

Luke, in his account in chapter four, verse forty and onward, says: "After nightfall, all who had sick friends suffering from various diseases brought them to Jesus. He laid His hands on each of them and healed them. Demons also came out of many people, shouting: "You are the Son of God!" They knew that Jesus was the Messiah, so He rebuked them and did not allow them to speak."

Jesus was not interested in becoming famous but in peacefully visiting all the regions of Israel. However, His fame soon became an obstacle to preaching the message of salvation and restoration.

Matthew says: "But this was to fulfill what was spoken by the prophet Isaiah: 'He took upon Himself our infirmities and bore our diseases.'"

Matthew recognized the fulfillment of this prophecy as Jesus healed the sick; it was as if He was taking their illnesses upon Himself. The rest of that prophecy was fulfilled on the cross. When Jesus took on sin, He truly bore the world's curse in His body.

What stood out to you the most?

_____

_____

_____

_____

_____

How can this reflection enhance your spiritual life?

_____

_____

_____

_____

_____

What would you say to Jesus today?

_____

_____

_____

_____

_____

*"For I am convinced that neither death nor life, neither
angels nor principalities, neither powers nor the present nor the
future, neither height nor depth, nor anything else in all
creation, will be able to separate us from the love of God
that is in Christ Jesus, our Lord."*
Romans 8:38-39

THE LEPER WHO KNEELS

He, covered by the impurity of leprosy, lived on the margins, without hope, separated from everyone. Yet Jesus, purity incarnate, reached out His hand, touched him, and transformed his pain into a miracle.

A leper came to Jesus, knelt before Him, and said:
— Lord, I know that You can heal me if You are willing.
Jesus had great compassion for him, reached out and touched him, and said:
— Yes! I am willing. You are healed.
At that moment, the leprosy disappeared, and he was healed. And Jesus clearly instructed him:
— Look! Don't tell anyone, but go to the priest and have him examine you. Then, to prove to everyone that you are healed, offer the sacrifice Moses commanded. After that, Jesus sent him away.
But the man went out and began to tell everyone what had happened. Because of this, in a short time, large crowds surrounded Jesus, and He could no longer enter any city publicly. And although He stayed in isolated places, people came to Him from all over.
Mark 1:40-44

According to the Mosaic Law, a Jew who touched a leper became ceremonially unclean, as described in Leviticus 13:45-46, 14:1-9. Leprosy was considered a grave impurity, and lepers were forced to live in isolation, far from the community. Anyone who touched them had to undergo purification rituals.

Jesus' action of touching the leper was, therefore, both surprising and scandalous by the religious standards of the time. However, instead of Jesus becoming impure, the leper became pure. This demonstrated Christ's divine power, showing that He not only healed physically but also restored spiritually those who were marginalized.

When we look at this man's story and understand the gravity of his condition, we realize how grand this miracle was in his life. Leprosy, in Jesus' day, was one of the worst diseases someone could have. It was not only a terminal illness but also a disease that separated the person from their family and society. A leper could not approach loved ones, work, or even stay in cities. Imagine being sick, hopeless, cut off from family, without friends, and forced to live in isolation.

In light of this reality, the man approached Jesus with humility and desperation. He knelt before Him and begged for healing. Luke's account of the story mentions that he fell on his face, which shows the depth of his pain and suffering.

The text tells us that Jesus, moved with compassion, reached out and healed him. Jesus instructed him not to spread the news, as He wanted to continue preaching in the towns, but the man couldn't contain his joy. He began to tell everyone about what had happened, which caused large crowds to gather around Jesus, making it difficult for Him to enter cities. As a result, He had to stay in isolated places, but still, people came to Him from everywhere.

An interesting point in this text is that leprosy at that time was seen as a curse from God, as if the person was being punished for sin. Many associated the disease with sin. Today, we know that leprosy, or Hansen's disease, is a chronic illness caused by a bacteria that affects nerves, causing loss of sensation and muscle strength, primarily affecting the eyes, arms, and legs. It is a terrible and progressive disease that gradually robs the person of their motor functions.

Despite the fact that this man had lost physical sensitivity, he did not lose his spiritual sensitivity. He recognized that Jesus had the answer to his problem. Perhaps he no longer felt his hands or was weak in his legs, but he had the faith to seek the only person who could transform his life.

The way he fell at Jesus' feet shows his desperation, as if it was his last chance for healing. He asked for help from the right person! When he came to Jesus, he found the One who could change his story.

Every time we go to Jesus, we are going to the One who can solve our problems. The joy of that man was so great that he couldn't keep it to himself. In a way, he impacted Jesus' ministry in that region because the fame of the miracles made it difficult for Him to continue entering cities and villages freely. Even so, how could anyone blame him? The blessing he received was so great that it was impossible to keep it to himself.

When God works a miracle in our lives, it becomes known to everyone around us. That man was condemned to a life of isolation and suffering, but he found in Jesus the hope he needed. Perhaps you feel like him, thinking that you've come to the end of the line, with no solution, no way out. Perhaps you're facing a problem that seems impossible to solve.

One of the reasons I decided to share this series on Jesus' miracles is to remind everyone how wonderful it is to trust in Him. My desire is that, as you listen to these reflections, you remember, understand, or learn that nothing is impossible for God. Through Jesus, everything is possible!

If Jesus performed this miracle for that man, He can do the same for you. God does not show favoritism. He loves you just as He loved that leper. When that man fell at Jesus' feet and said, "If You are willing, You can make me clean," Jesus responded: "I am willing; be clean." When Jesus touched that man, He transformed that illness into health and took away all the curse that the disease brought.

When he left there, I imagine that the first thing he did, after meeting with the priest, was to seek out his family. How many hugs that were once forbidden, now could be experienced and cherished.

What stood out to you the most?

_____

_____

_____

_____

_____

How can this reflection enhance your spiritual life?

_____

_____

_____

_____

_____

What would you say to Jesus today?

_____

_____

_____

_____

_____

_____

"The thief comes only to steal and kill and destroy; I have come that they may have life, and have it to the full."
John 10:10

THE PARALYZED MAN FROM THE ROOF

A group of men used their faith boldly, breaking barriers and challenging limitations. They thought beyond the obvious, demonstrating creativity combined with faith.

One day Jesus was teaching, and some Pharisees and teachers of the Law were sitting near him. They had come from all the towns of Galilee and Judea and also from Jerusalem. The power of the Lord was with Jesus to heal the sick. Some men brought a paralytic lying on a bed and were trying to get into the house to place him before Jesus. However, because of the crowd, they could not get in with the paralytic. So they carried him up to the roof. They made an opening in the tiles and lowered him on his bed in front of Jesus, in the midst of the people who were there. Jesus saw that they had faith and said to the paralytic:

— My friend, your sins are forgiven!

The teachers of the Law and the Pharisees began to think:

— Who is this man who blasphemes against God in this way? No one can forgive sins; only God has this power.

But Jesus knew what they were thinking and said:

— Why are you thinking like this? What is easier to say to the paralytic: "Your sins are forgiven" or "Get up and walk"? But I will show you that I, the Son of Man, have authority on earth to forgive sins.

Then he said to the paralytic:

— I tell you: get up, take your bed, and go home.

At once the man got up in front of everyone, took his bed, and went home, praising God. Everyone was amazed and, filled with fear, praised God, saying:

— What an amazing thing we have seen today!

Luke 5:17-26

This miracle is about a paralyzed man who, in the time of Jesus, lived in a miserable situation because he couldn't work and depended on alms or his family's support. It was a terrible condition for anyone. Despite the difficulties and the human impossibility of solving this problem, his friends believed that Jesus could perform the miracle.

This text speaks about many things: the Pharisees, the scribes, the crowd, and the context of the story. However, something interesting is that the paralyzed man's name is not mentioned. The writer of the text didn't record his name, but I'm sure he didn't mind, as he left there with his miracle.

Some interesting points, common to the miracles of Jesus, are:

Faith: Most of the people who received miracles had faith.

Action: They took action to receive the miracle.

Courage: This miracle, in particular, required courage. Those men faced ridicule because it had never been seen before for someone to lower a sick person through the roof. The crowds around Jesus were so large that they needed to be creative. They were not ashamed to pursue the miracle.

Sometimes, we need miracles but are ashamed to cry out, to humble ourselves before God, or to correct our paths to receive them. Those men were not ashamed. They were absolutely sure that Jesus could heal the paralytic. They thought: "If we put our friend before Jesus, he will be healed." They saw no obstacle. They climbed onto the roof, lowered the paralytic, and placed him before Jesus, and He, seeing their faith, healed the man.

This teaches us that we need faith without doubts. We need to believe that Jesus is powerful enough to forgive sins, heal, deliver, and change our lives. What miracle do you need? I also need miracles, and the hope I have is that we can grow in faith. How? Faith comes by hearing the Word of God. If your faith is small, listen more to the Word, meditate on God's promises, and believe. Your faith will grow in your heart, and you will receive your miracle.

If we could highlight one point of this miracle, it would be that those men were absolutely sure that Jesus would heal. Based on this, I ask some important questions:

What has been your attitude to receive your miracle?

Are you persevering or have you given up? Have you stopped praying, seeking, or believing? As those men carried the paralytic, they said to him, "Don't worry, we will put you before Jesus, and He will heal you!" With every step, their faith increased. To receive a miracle, you will face challenges. Perhaps the first will be the disbelief of family, friends, or colleagues. When you say, "I want to be promoted," they may reply, "But you don't have the qualifications!" Or, as they told those men: "You won't be able to reach Jesus!" Yet they looked at the roof and thought: "It's possible to go that way!" God has a path for your miracle. For Him, nothing is impossible.

Do you have the courage to face difficulties and receive your miracle?

What difficulties are you facing? You will need faith, courage, and perseverance to keep seeking.

Where is your faith?

Is your faith in men, science, probabilities, or in the God of the impossible? If I were you, I would place my faith in the same person those men trusted: Jesus. He is the one who forgives sins, heals, delivers, and performs miracles. This is our God!

The moral of this story is that there is no difficulty that can prevent you from receiving your miracle. Those men had the mindset that nothing would stop them from reaching the presence of Jesus. If you believe, you will see the glory of God. John 11:40

What stood out to you the most?

_____

_____

_____

_____

_____

How can this reflection enhance your spiritual life?

_____

_____

_____

_____

What would you say to Jesus today?

_____

_____

_____

_____

_____

_____

_____

"The righteous cry out, and the Lord hears them; he delivers them from all their troubles."
Psalm 34:17

THE PARALYZED MAN OF BETHESDA

While many say that hope is slow to die, this man never gave up waiting. In the midst of celebration, he lived in sorrow and sickness, waiting for his miracle. His perseverance is a testimony of faith, even when everything around him seemed far from healing and joy.

After this, there was a Jewish feast, and Jesus went up to Jerusalem. There is a pool in Jerusalem near the Sheep Gate, which has five covered colonnades. In Hebrew it is called Bethesda. Around these colonnades lay a great number of sick people: the blind, the lame, and the paralyzed. [They were waiting for the movement of the water, because from time to time an angel of the Lord would come down and stir up the water. The first one to enter the pool after the water was stirred would be healed of whatever disease they had.] Among them was a man who had been sick for thirty-eight years. Jesus saw him lying there and knew that he had been in that condition for a long time, so he asked him:
— Do you want to be healed?
He answered:
— Sir, I have no one to put me into the pool when the water is stirred. Every time I try to go in, someone else goes down ahead of me.
Then Jesus said:
— Get up, pick up your mat, and walk!
At once the man was healed. He picked up his mat and began to walk. This happened on a Sabbath. Because of this, the Jewish leaders said to him:
— Today is the Sabbath, and our Law does not allow you to carry your mat.
He replied:
— The man who healed me told me, "Pick up your mat and walk."
They asked him:
— Who is the man who told you to do this?
But the man did not know who it was, for Jesus had slipped away into the crowd that was there.
Later Jesus found him at the Temple and said to him:

— Listen! You are now healed. Do not sin anymore, so that nothing worse may happen to you.
The man went away and told the Jewish leaders that it was Jesus who had healed him. So they began to persecute Jesus because he had done this healing on the Sabbath.
Then Jesus said to them:
— My Father is always working until now, and I too am working.
Because of this, the Jewish leaders tried all the more to kill him. Not only was he breaking the Sabbath, but he was also calling God his own Father, making himself equal with God. John 5:1-18

This miracle is one of the longest, as it can be divided into two parts: the performance of the miracle and the political-religious conflict between Jesus and the Pharisees. The focus here will be only on the first part, the miracle itself, which is the most relevant to us.

That man had been lying by the pool of Bethesda for thirty-eight years. He did not know Jesus, did not recognize Him, and had not gone in search of Him. In many other miracles, people came to Jesus ready to receive their healing. They had heard about Him and came full of faith in their hearts; some even took action in pursuit of a miracle. This man, however, didn't.

Perhaps that is why he remained sick for thirty-eight years: he was not seeking God but had placed his hope in the pool. What qualified this man to receive the miracle? He didn't know the Word, he didn't recognize Jesus, and even with the living Word before him, he didn't know how to call upon it.

Jesus, being the Word made flesh, simply wanted to hear the man say "I want to," and the healing would happen. Yet the man didn't understand Jesus' question. When Jesus asked him if he wanted to be healed, he answered by explaining how hard it was for him to get into the pool, showing that he still didn't realize who was standing before him.

Perhaps he had never heard of Jesus, or if he had, he didn't know exactly who He was. The proof is that, when the Pharisees asked who had healed him, he simply answered that he didn't know. Only later, when he met Jesus again in the temple, did he realize it had been Him and then went to inform the Jews. From this, I realized there was only one quality in that man that qualified him for the miracle: perseverance.

He stayed there for thirty-eight years, believing that one day he would be healed. As a paralytic, he could have lived off alms anywhere in the city, but he chose to stay by that pool, week after week, day after day, waiting for his miracle. That perseverance caught Jesus' attention.

When Jesus looked at him, He saw that he had been in that condition for a long time. Through his clothes, his face, his sadness, Jesus knew the man had been waiting for years. Maybe during that time many had said to him, "You'll never be healed because you have no one to help you." Over the years, he began to believe that. Still, he kept going back to the pool.

The big issue was that the paralytic had faith in the pool, not in God. He waited for many years because he believed healing would come from that water. If he had placed his faith in God, would he have waited so long? How often do we also wait for a miracle in the way we want, the way we imagine? However, the miracle doesn't always come in our way, because it needs to be a blessing in our lives, not a curse.

Sometimes we ask God for something and think that only the miracle will solve our situation. However, if it wouldn't be a blessing for us, God won't give it to us. Because everything that comes from God is good, perfect, pleasant, enriches, and adds no sorrow. If the miracle we are asking for doesn't have these characteristics, then it's not God's will for us.

In the paralytic's case, his healing was a blessing. Still, he waited so many years because he had placed his faith in the wrong place. If it weren't for Jesus' mercy, he would never have received his healing. Many sick people were there, yet Jesus spoke directly to that paralytic. His condition drew the Lord's mercy.

We notice that even after healing him, Jesus still gave him advice for his personal life and warned him not to sin anymore so that something worse wouldn't happen to him. What could be worse for a man who had been sick for so long? The worst thing that can happen to someone is to die without God. Jesus warned him because He knew that after so long in that condition, the man might be tempted to make up for lost time and end up sinning. Truly, that man received two great opportunities from God: one for physical healing and another through a powerful piece of advice for his life.

Today, we constantly have God's mercy upon us, and His Word guides us to overcome in every area of our lives. Every time we read His Word and listen to His counsel, it is as if Jesus Himself were by our side, guiding and advising us. May we have discernment to place our faith in God and not in other resources. May we be ready to receive God's will for our lives, so that we don't have to wait thirty-eight years for a miracle. If we could draw one key lesson from this miracle, it would be this: never give up on your miracle, no matter how long or difficult it may seem. Even in the face of hardship, that paralytic never gave up. He always returned to the pool, waiting for his miracle.

Today, however, we don't need to go to a pool or any specific place; we only need to go to Jesus, because He is the source of life and the reason for our miracles.

What stood out to you the most?

_____

_____

_____

_____

_____

How can this reflection enhance your spiritual life?

_____

_____

_____

_____

What would you say to Jesus today?

_____

_____

_____

_____

_____

"Do not be anxious about anything, but in everything, by prayer and supplication with thanksgiving, let your requests be made known to God; and the peace of God, which surpasses all understanding, will guard your hearts and your minds in Christ Jesus."

Philippians 4:6-7

THE MAN'S HAND

Among many miracles, this one stands out for its simplicity and depth. On the Sabbath, inside the synagogue, Jesus heals a man without him asking or showing faith. This act reveals divine mercy, the sovereignty of Christ, and the priority of love over religious rules.

On another Sabbath, Jesus went into the synagogue and began to teach. There was a man there whose right hand was crippled. Some people, who wanted to accuse Jesus of disobeying the Law, asked Him:
— Is it against our Law to heal on the Sabbath?
Jesus replied:
— If one of you has a sheep and it falls into a pit on the Sabbath, won't he do everything to pull it out? A person is worth much more than a sheep. Therefore, our Law allows us to help others on the Sabbath.
Then He said to the man:
— Stretch out your hand!
He stretched it out, and it was healed and became just like the other one.
Then the Pharisees who were there went out and began to make plans to kill Jesus.
Luke 6:6, Matthew 12:10b

This miracle happens on a Sabbath, inside a synagogue, and the religious people always prioritized religion over doing good. According to Jewish law, it was forbidden to exert effort, work, or even cook on the Sabbath. To this day, orthodox Jews do none of these things on the Sabbath. They have a specific distance they are allowed to walk, and nothing is done at home. Anything that involves effort is prohibited because the Sabbath is a day of total rest.

They already knew that Jesus healed on every day of the week. They also knew He healed on the Sabbath. So they were just waiting for Jesus to perform a healing in order to accuse Him of breaking the Sabbath.

However, Jesus did not break the Sabbath, because He did not exert any physical effort. The only thing He used was His words. Jesus went even further to explain that, according to the law, any of them could rescue an animal in distress without breaking the law. So Jesus questioned them in this way: "Well, you can save an animal, but you can't save a man? You can do good for an animal, but you can't do good for a person?"

If it were me, I would justify it differently. I would say, "I'm using the same breath to heal this man as I am to talk to you. How can that be breaking the Sabbath?" But Jesus chose to do it this way. Who am I to disagree with Jesus?

The most important part of this miracle is not the religious or legal side of the story. The most interesting part, for me, is who receives the healing, who receives the blessing. In the end, that man left his house in the morning one way, under a curse, and came back under a blessing. That, to me, is the most important thing.

Analyzing the text, I see that, unlike other miracles, this man didn't need anything that many others did. He did nothing, believed nothing, didn't humble himself in any way, and made no effort to seek out Jesus or beg Him. This is one of the shortest miracles in the Bible, but very interesting because it's so different from many others.

This man left home in the morning like someone who walks out with a check in his pocket. If someone asked him, "Do you have money?" he would say, "Yes." But if they asked, "Where is it?" he'd reply, "It's in the bank. I'm going to withdraw it now." The blessing was already prepared, waiting for him. This man left home sick, but in the spiritual world, he had already received the miracle, without even knowing it, but God knew.

He didn't need faith, action, or humility. He simply was at the right place, at the right time, in the presence of the right person. These three factors were decisive because he was in the synagogue exactly on the day when Jesus would demonstrate that saving a human life is more important than preserving an animal. That man did nothing. Isn't it often like that in our own lives? We receive so many things from God without doing anything—simply through His mercy. Every day we receive deliverance, daily bread, and countless blessings from the Lord without doing anything to deserve them. However, God acts like this: "I want to bless you, and you will be blessed." The only thing that man did was obey Jesus. When Jesus said, "Stretch out your hand," he obeyed.

So even though he didn't have faith, action, or humility, in the end, he obeyed the voice of Jesus. That's the secret! Even if you don't have enough faith, even if you're not ready yet, obey the voice of the Lord. Believe what Jesus is saying to you. Even if your faith is not at its highest level, even if you don't feel ready, even if it's not because of your sacrifice—listen to what Jesus has for your life.

He only needed to be in the presence of Jesus and come into contact with His healing anointing. That is what we need: to be in the presence of the Lord so we can receive His anointing for our lives. There is an anointing for us, a blessing set apart for each person in Christ Jesus. The only thing we need is to believe in the word of Jesus and in the One who sent Him in order to have eternal life. If we have a covenant with God through Jesus, our life is transformed. With this covenant the benefits are greater. With the covenant the protection is guaranteed.

There is a great difference between those who have a covenant with God and those who do not. In the end, that difference will be even clearer: the one who serves God and the one who doesn't, the one who has a covenant and the one who doesn't. God wants to make a covenant with you today. He wants to renew His vows with you today. Do you know why? Because there are many things God wants to do in your life, but He can't because your covenant with Him is broken, stained, or perhaps it doesn't even exist. That man had Abraham's covenant upon him and was in God's house, even with all his problems. Maybe he never expected to be healed that way, but God's grace reached him that Sabbath morning.

Jesus preached, "Come to Me, come to Me, come to Me." That's what He's saying to you today: "Come! I have life and life in abundance for you!" However, you need to make a decision so that your life changes. I assure you that when you align your covenant with God, you step into the position to receive benefits you did nothing to deserve—but you become qualified to receive them.

The key point of this miracle, is that the man did nothing to deserve it. Do you know what I understood from that? When God is going to give you a miracle, nothing can prevent you from receiving it. Jesus decided to heal him, and it would not be religion, the Sabbath, the law, faith, or the condition of that man that would prevent the healing.

Enter into a covenant with God so you can receive everything He has prepared for you without needing to understand or question why you're receiving so many blessings. When you get home after a long, tiring day and lay your head down to rest, you can think: "I made it through another day. I got home safely, I have food and drink in the fridge, water to bathe and relax from the daily stress, a bed to sleep in, and a roof to shelter me." Even if you don't have any of that, know this: there's a night between your day of defeat and a new day to try again and achieve your victory.

What stood out to you the most?

_____

_____

_____

_____

_____

How can this reflection enhance your spiritual life?

_____

_____

_____

_____

_____

What would you say to Jesus today?

_____

_____

_____

_____

_____

"And whatever you ask in My name, I will do it, that the Father may be glorified in the Son. If you ask anything in My name, I will do it."
John 14:13-14

THE PROPHECY

After a miracle on the Sabbath, Jesus faces fierce opposition from the Pharisees, who plot against Him. Even though He is threatened, He withdraws, but His compassion does not fade. He continues to heal the sick, revealing a love that transcends hatred and persecution.

Then the Pharisees who were there went out and began to plot to kill Jesus. When Jesus learned of this, He left that place, and many people followed Him. He healed all those who were sick and ordered them not to tell anyone about Him. This happened to fulfill what the prophet Isaiah had said:
"God said: Here is my chosen servant, the one I love, who brings great joy to my heart. I will put my Spirit on Him, and He will announce my judgment to all the nations. He will not argue, or shout, or make speeches in the streets. He will not crush the bruised reed, nor put out the smoldering wick. He will act this way until justice prevails. And all the nations will put their hope in Him." Matthew 12:14-21

This episode reveals not only the power and mercy of Christ but also the fulfillment of the Scriptures, showing that He was the Servant chosen by God. The Pharisees were religious leaders strict in observing the Law and saw Jesus as a threat to their control over the people. The healing on the Sabbath, considered a violation of Jewish law, intensified their hatred toward Him, leading them to plan His death. Despite this, Jesus did not directly confront His opponents but withdrew, following the divine plan. Matthew associates this moment with the prophecy of Isaiah, highlighting the meek and compassionate character of the Messiah, who would not seek human recognition but would fulfill His mission with justice and mercy.

The prophecy reveals the messianic identity of Jesus as God's Servant, filled with the Holy Spirit, who came to restore the weak and bring hope to all nations. His attitude of not seeking conflict and continuing His work in silence reflects His divine nature and how the Kingdom of God operates—not through imposition but through love and justice. Some important points stand out:

They began to plot to kill Jesus

Jesus does not retaliate against the persecution but acts with wisdom, retreating to continue His mission. This teaches us that, in the face of opposition, we must trust in God's purpose and remain firm, not discouraged.

The command not to disclose the miracles

Jesus frequently asked for discretion regarding His deeds. This could have several reasons: to avoid a distorted view of His role as Messiah, to prevent the authorities from accelerating their persecution, and to keep the focus on His teachings, not just the miracles. The Synoptic Gospels record at least six occasions where Jesus instructed that His miracles not be disclosed.

He healed everyone

Jesus continues to heal those who follow Him, revealing that His compassion and power remain unwavering, regardless of circumstances. This teaches us that no matter the difficulties, He extends His hands with grace and love, without distinction between people. In six occasions, we see Jesus healing everyone. Only where there was unbelief did He not perform great miracles.

He will not crush the bruised reed

In the symbolism of this text, the "bruised reed" represents those who are wounded, rejected, and left aside by society. Although He announces God's judgment, Jesus did not come to condemn but to save, restore, and rescue all who are lost.

Nor put out the smoldering wick

The "smoldering wick" symbolizes someone who once had their faith or spiritual passion ablaze but is now weakened, with only a faint sign of spiritual life remaining. This wick can be compared to a person on the brink of spiritual death. In biblical times, the lamp was the main source of light, and we can use it as an example to understand this metaphor. A wick almost extinguished, with a faint flame, can still be reignited.

Jesus declared, "I am the light of the world. Whoever follows me will never walk in darkness but will have the light of life." John 8:12.

This miracle goes beyond physical healing. It shows the resistance of the Pharisees, the humility of Jesus, and the fulfillment of the Scriptures. We learn that the Kingdom of God is not imposed by force but by love, justice, and obedience to the Father's will.

The people who followed Him recognized His power and authority over diseases and evil spirits. As people were healed, His fame grew, and many others came to join the crowds. Even though He asked them not to disclose anything about Him, it didn't happen, and everyone wanted to meet the prophet who taught with authority and healed all.

What stood out to you the most?

_____

_____

_____

_____

_____

How can this reflection enhance your spiritual life?

_____

_____

_____

_____

What would you say to Jesus today?

_____

_____

_____

_____

_____

_____

"Peace I leave with you; my peace I give to you; not as the world gives do I give to you. Let not your heart be troubled, neither let it be afraid. You have heard me say to you, I am going away, and coming back to you."

John 14:27-28

THE CENTURION'S SERVANT

A Roman officer, with one hundred men under his command, bows in humility, seeking Jesus for the one he loved. Matthew and Luke tell us about this miracle, where the power of faith surpasses human authority, and healing comes through trust in the Lord.

When Jesus had finished saying these things to the crowd, He went to the town of Capernaum. There was a Roman centurion there who had a servant he valued greatly. The servant was very sick, almost dying. When the officer heard about Jesus, he sent some Jewish leaders to ask Him to come and heal his servant. They went to speak with Jesus and earnestly requested:

— This man deserves Your help, for he loves our people and even built a synagogue for us. So Jesus went with them. However, when He was already near the house, the Roman officer sent some friends to say to Jesus:

— Lord, do not trouble Yourself, for I am not worthy to have You come under my roof. And I also think I am not worthy of the honor of speaking to You in person. Just give the order, and my servant will be healed. I too am under the authority of superior officers, and I have soldiers who obey my commands. I say to one, "Go," and he goes. I say to another, "Come," and he comes. And I say to my servant, "Do this," and he does it.

When Jesus heard this, He was amazed and said to those following Him:

— I tell you the truth, I have never found such great faith, not even in Israel! I tell you that many will come from the East and the West and will sit at the table in the Kingdom of Heaven with Abraham, Isaac, and Jacob. But the subjects of the Kingdom will be thrown outside, into the darkness, where there will be weeping and gnashing of teeth.

Then Jesus said to the officer: Go back home, because it will be done as you have believed. And at that moment, the Roman officer's servant was healed. Luke 7:1-9

When Jesus admired the faith of the centurion, He recognized not only the man's belief in His restorative power but also his deep understanding of faith. The centurion saw that faith knows no boundaries, not even the boundary of distance. By comparing his own authority to the obedience of his soldiers, he seemed to view faith as a servant of the Lord, ready to obey whatever He commanded. If my servant obeys me, why wouldn't faith obey You?

The centurion also humbled himself, acknowledging that he was not worthy for Jesus to enter his home. This is a rare quality among men of authority and leadership. Humility is often seen as weakness or insecurity, but the centurion was unbothered by this perception.

Though the text doesn't reveal much about the centurion's personal character, the context speaks volumes. The Jewish leaders went to Jesus to give a good testimony about the man's generosity, having built a synagogue for the people. In the end, even Jesus gave a good testimony about him.

The text doesn't specify what kind of servant was sick. He could have been a member of the centurion's guard or someone assisting him at home. All we know is that the servant was dearly loved. The centurion's love reminds me of the love and care of the Good Shepherd in the parable, who leaves the ninety-nine sheep to seek the one that was lost. Both had a hundred, but for just one, they left everything behind to search for salvation.

The Good Shepherd in the parable symbolizes God the Father, who does everything to recover His lost sheep. Jesus was sent by the Father to rescue us. The centurion could have easily replaced the servant in his household, just as the shepherd could have found another sheep to replace the lost one. However, the uniqueness of each living being makes all the difference. Another servant wouldn't be the same beloved servant; another sheep wouldn't be the same precious sheep.

Have you ever reflected on your own uniqueness? Among all the beings in the universe, there has never been and never will be anyone exactly like you. Perhaps this is why Jesus loved everyone equally, without making distinctions between the poor and the rich, the wise and the foolish, the healed or the sick. Jesus often praised the faith of those who displayed unwavering trust in His power and authority, as He did with the centurion. If He looked at our faith today, would He consider it admirable or small?

Jesus wanted to show that true faith isn't limited to those who were born into Israel or who have a religious heritage, but is recognized and valued by God regardless of origin. By praising the centurion's faith, He highlighted that this unwavering trust surpassed even the faith He found among the people of Israel. Furthermore, by saying, "many will come from the East and West and will sit at the table in the Kingdom of Heaven," Jesus was prophesying that access to the Kingdom would not be restricted to an exclusive group but would be open to all who demonstrate true faith.

On the other hand, those who, though part of Israel, did not recognize or cultivate this faith would be rejected, resulting in spiritual condemnation described as a place of sadness, where "there will be weeping and gnashing of teeth in despair." In essence, Jesus was teaching that salvation depends on authentic faith and that God values those who believe, regardless of their background. Mere affiliation is insufficient if it is accompanied by disbelief.

What stood out to you the most?

_____

_____

_____

_____

_____

How can this reflection enhance your spiritual life?

_____

_____

_____

_____

What would you say to Jesus today?

_____

_____

_____

_____

_____

*"And Jesus answered them, saying, have faith in God.
For truly I say to you, whoever says to this mountain, 'Be taken
up and thrown into the sea,' and does not doubt in his heart,
but believes that what he says will come to
pass, it will be done for him."*
Mark 11:22-24

THE WIDOW'S SON

On the path of sorrow, death meets the author of life. Luke narrates the story of a widow whose lament turned into joy. The touch of Jesus' compassion restored her hope, changing her life forever.

A short time later Jesus went to a town called Nain. His disciples and a large crowd went with him. As he was approaching the town gate, a funeral procession was coming out. The dead man was the only son of a widow, and a large group of people from the city was with her. When the Lord saw her, he was filled with compassion and said:
— Do not cry.
Then he came closer and touched the coffin. The men carrying it stopped. Then Jesus said:
— Young man, I command you: get up!
The young man sat up in the coffin and began to speak, and Jesus gave him back to his mother.
Everyone was filled with great fear and praised God, saying:
— A great prophet has appeared among us! God has come to save his people!
This news about Jesus spread throughout the whole country and the surrounding regions. Luke 7:11

This miracle took place in the town of Nain, involving a widow who had lost her son. As I observe this story, I notice a few details: the crowd, the death, the sorrow, the buried dreams, and the tears. That was what was happening at that moment, in that city, to that family – a widow with an only son.

A crowd followed the funeral, but perhaps few people had been there at the birth of that boy. In sorrow, everyone gathered to share her grief, unlike in our lives, where it is often hard to find people willing to celebrate our joy.

That crowd was there to share the sorrow of that woman. Since she was a widow and had only that son, it is likely she had already buried all her dreams before burying her son – dreams of seeing him grow, of having a larger family, grandchildren, of prospering. Without the workforce of children, her future would be to live off alms or depend on the help of the synagogue.

When things seem hopeless and you see no way out, it becomes very easy to give up. That woman certainly had no hope of seeing her son alive again. You know what? Where Jesus passes by, sorrow goes away. Sorrow cannot remain in the presence of the Lord Jesus. We see, miracle after miracle, that Jesus felt deep compassion. That compassion is our hope, because our God has compassion for us.

When Jesus approached her, the first thing He said was not: "I will bring your son back to life," but: "Do not cry." Wouldn't it have been easier for Jesus to simply say He would restore her son's life? However, He did it differently. First, He told her not to cry, then He performed the miracle. That's what God is telling you today: do not cry, because He has deep compassion for you, regardless of the problem you are facing.

Jesus always says "Do not cry" before performing a miracle. Do you know why? Because it is necessary to believe in Him. When He said that to the woman, it was as if He were saying: "Believe in Me, for I will solve your problems; I will resurrect not only your son but also your dreams, your hope, and your future." Imagine someone in a funeral procession, and as they pass by someone else, that person holds the coffin and says: "Stop, you're not going to the cemetery." It was something like that Jesus did: He stopped the procession and spoke to the woman. Many times, we are walking toward places that Jesus does not want for us. He invites us to leave our tears behind, for He can transform our life, restore our dreams, and solve our problems. That act of not crying is a sign of faith and hope, because Jesus is our hope.

The people were amazed at the power of Jesus and asked: "What great prophet has appeared among us!" That day, the woman went back home not with a coffin, but with her son in her arms. Jesus will always reach us with deep compassion. Will you listen to what Jesus has to say or will you keep crying, lamenting, without hope? There are those who prefer to continue crying, but it is never too late to realize that life in Christ still offers hope.

The people were amazed at Jesus' power, but what about you – have you been amazed at the power He has to change your story? That crowd was amazed because they saw the miracle. You must be amazed by faith. In the end, Jesus wants to surprise you, to make you say: "My Jesus, how good You are!" Thank You, Jesus, for the miracle. The same Jesus who worked the miracle for the widow of Nain is with us today and ready to perform miracles in our lives.

Our life may be like a funeral procession, carrying the remains of dreams, hopes, and vitality we once had, but that were shaken by the weight of sin or sorrow. Just as in the story where the widow carried the coffin of her son, we too may, at some point, carry the feeling of inner sadness, of a slumbering spirit.

Then, Jesus comes near us with compassion. He says to us: "Do not cry." With a touch full of authority and love, He interrupts the course of spiritual death and calls us to rise, and in an instant, like the man who sat up and spoke, we are reborn, not only physically healed, but spiritually restored. Upon receiving the miracle, we leave behind the burden of sadness and hopelessness and begin to live with the vitality and hope that only Jesus can offer. Just as the widow was filled with joy to see her son alive again, we too find, in the presence of the Savior, the renewal of life and the recovery of all we thought we had lost.

What stood out to you the most?

_____

_____

_____

_____

_____

How can this reflection enhance your spiritual life?

_____

_____

_____

_____

What would you say to Jesus today?

_____

_____

_____

_____

_____

"Blessed be the God and Father of our Lord Jesus
Christ, who has blessed us with every spiritual blessing
in the heavenly realms in Christ"
Ephesians 1:3

THE SINFUL WOMAN

Only God can do the impossible. Forgiving sins is a divine miracle, an act of unconditional love. The story of the woman who received this miracle is a testimony of the grace that transforms lives.

A Pharisee invited Jesus to have dinner. Jesus went to his house and sat down to eat. In that city lived a sinful woman. She found out that Jesus was dining at the Pharisee's house. So she took a jar made of alabaster, full of perfume, and stood behind Jesus at his feet. She was crying, and her tears were wetting his feet. Then she wiped them with her own hair. She kissed Jesus' feet and poured the perfume on them. When the Pharisee saw this, he thought to himself: "If this man really were a prophet, he would know who this woman is who is touching him and the sinful life she leads."

Jesus then said to the Pharisee:

— Simon, I have something to tell you:

— Speak, Master! — Simon replied.

Jesus said:

— Two men owed money to a man who used to lend money. One owed him five hundred silver coins, and the other fifty, but neither of them could pay back what they owed. So the lender forgave both debts. Which one will love him more?

— I suppose it's the one who had the bigger debt forgiven! — Simon answered.

— You're right! — Jesus said.

Then he turned toward the woman and said to Simon:

— Do you see this woman? When I came in, you didn't offer me water to wash my feet, but she washed them with her tears and dried them with her hair. You didn't greet me with a kiss when I arrived; but she hasn't stopped kissing my feet since I came in. You didn't put perfumed oil on my head, but she poured perfume on my feet. I tell you, then, the great love she has shown proves

that her many sins have already been forgiven. But where little is forgiven, little love is shown.
Then Jesus said to the woman:
— Your sins are forgiven.
Those sitting at the table began to ask: Who is this man who even forgives sins?
But Jesus said to the woman:
— Your faith has saved you. Go in peace.
    Luke 7:36-50

Before we reflect on the story of this woman, we need to understand the Greek word used for "sinner" (hamartolos – G268), which Luke uses to identify her. This word is used forty-five times in the New Testament to refer to sinners in general. Since she was a woman, it is believed that she openly committed sins considered despicable by the Jewish community. Jesus causes three scandals among those men: possibly not being a true prophet for not knowing the woman's sinful life; allowing the woman to touch Him, as Jewish tradition did not accept women touching men outside of family relationships; and forgiving her sins.

The Three Scandals

The doubt about His prophetic identity

The Pharisees and other religious leaders of that time believed that a true prophet would have discernment about people's character and lives. When Jesus allowed a sinful woman to approach Him and touch Him, it raised questions: "If He were really a prophet, He would know who she is and what kind of life she leads" (Luke 7:39). For those men, the fact that Jesus did not reject her was a sign that He did not possess the divine knowledge expected from a messenger of God. However, Jesus not only knew the condition of that woman, but He saw beyond her reputation; He saw a repentant heart ready to receive forgiveness.

63

Breaking social and religious norms

In first-century Jewish culture, there were strict rules about the interaction between men and women, especially those who were not from the same family. A woman touching a man in public was considered improper, even more so if that woman had a questionable reputation. When Jesus allowed her to touch Him and anoint His feet, He scandalized the religious leaders, as He violated social conventions and demonstrated a love and acceptance that went beyond human rules. This act of Jesus teaches us that God's mercy is not limited by traditions or appearances but reaches everyone.

The power to forgive sins

The greatest scandal of all was Jesus declaring forgiveness to that woman. The Pharisees believed that only God had the authority to forgive sins, and hearing Jesus pronounce words of absolution sounded like blasphemy. To them, this was an affront to divine authority and the law. However, Jesus not only granted forgiveness but did so with full authority, showing that He was more than a prophet: He was the very Son of God. This moment revealed that the real scandal was not the woman's presence, but the hardening of the hearts of those men who could not recognize the Messiah before them.

Upon learning of Jesus' location, that woman decided to turn to repentance. I imagine that with every step she took toward the Pharisee's house, her heart grew anxious and tight, fearing rejection and being thrown out. Still, the reception that Jesus gave her was that of a beloved daughter.

This woman's attitude teaches us that true repentance leads us to the presence of Jesus with humility and total surrender. Her tears were not a sign of hopeless despair but an expression of a heart that found forgiveness and redemption. While the Pharisees despised her, Jesus valued her and declared her salvation: "Your sins are forgiven. Your faith has saved you; go in peace."

What stood out to you the most?

_____

_____

_____

_____

_____

How can this reflection enhance your spiritual life?

_____

_____

_____

_____

What would you say to Jesus today?

_____

_____

_____

_____

_____

*"Jesus answered them, 'Most assuredly, I say to you,
whoever commits sin is a slave of sin. And a slave does not abide
in the house forever, but a son abides forever. Therefore, if the
Son makes you free, you shall be free indeed."*
John 8:34-36

THE BLIND AND MUTE

In the shadows of a silent and colorless world, he wandered, lost in solitude. His eyes were now mere mirrors of darkness. His lips were bound in a deep silence, as if the very air had forgotten the words.

Then they brought to Jesus a man who was blind and mute because he was possessed by a demon. Jesus healed him, and he began to see and speak. The crowd was amazed and asked:
— Could this be the Son of David?
But some Pharisees heard this and said:
— It is by Beelzebul, the prince of demons, that this man casts out demons.
But Jesus knew their thoughts and said:
— A nation divided into groups that fight against each other will certainly be destroyed. A city or a family divided into groups that fight each other will also be destroyed. So if Satan's kingdom is divided and one group fights against another, that means his kingdom is already falling apart and will soon be finished. You say I cast out demons by the power of Beelzebul. But if that's true, who gives your followers the power to cast them out? Your own followers prove that you are completely mistaken. In fact, it is by the power of God that I cast out demons, and this proves that the Kingdom of God has already come to you.
Matthew 12:22-28

The blind man regained his sight and speech, but that miracle was not enough to convince the Pharisees about who Jesus was. The people were as blind as that man once had been. The man spoke again because he was freed from the evil spirit; yet the religious men, who could speak, uttered blasphemies, so it would have been better if they had never been able to say a word.

This episode actually reveals not only a man enslaved by an evil spirit who could not see or speak, but also the spiritual blindness of many who were witnessing the event. It is important to notice how the crowd reacted to everything Jesus did in front of them. They saw a tremendous miracle: the man who could not speak or see was delivered. That alone should have been enough for everyone to believe that Jesus was the Messiah, the Son of God sent from above.

The miracles Jesus performed had never been seen before: miracle after miracle, He proved who He was. However, the people's unbelief was so great that even in the face of something extraordinary, they still asked Jesus for a greater sign, a sign from heaven, to see if they could believe.

Sometimes Jesus rebuked them, calling them a "wicked generation." He said that the only sign given to them would be the sign of Jonah, who spent three days and three nights in the belly of the great fish. In the same way, the Son of Man would spend three days and three nights in the heart of the earth. He would not give any more signs besides those that were already being done.

What we understand is that unbelief is a barrier that blocks understanding. They saw but could not perceive. They looked, but their hearts did not believe. Isn't the same true for us? When we go through trials, struggles or difficulties, we start questioning the Lord. We ask if He loves us, if He will care for us, if He will perform the miracle. Where is the Lord? These are the questions we ask.

There is no one who hasn't asked this question at some point. When we face hardship, the first reaction is to ask: "Why is this happening to me? I'm not a bad person. Why do I have to go through this?" That's called life. Life is not predictable but unpredictable, and that's what makes it so interesting. If it were completely planned, it wouldn't be enjoyable. Life is surprising. We know what is now and what was yesterday, but tomorrow— we know nothing about.

Often, we ask God the same questions: "Give me a sign, Lord. Give me a sign!" Hasn't Jesus already given us enough signs to believe in Him? If you have any doubt, your faith is not perfect.

If you think God has abandoned you, your faith is not perfect. If you think of failure, your faith is not yet perfected in love.

These people saw the miracles but couldn't believe. Not all of them, of course, because the Word says that many were amazed while others asked for more signs. Jesus, later on, also explains what happens with people who are bound and tormented by evil spirits. He doesn't speak directly but uses a figure of speech, comparing the man to a house, a temple. When this temple is clean and empty, the spirits return. They bring more spirits, worse than the first, and the final condition of the person without God becomes worse than the first.

If they had asked that man what he thought about Jesus, if He really was a prophet, the Messiah sent by God, he surely would have said that he was blind and now could see, mute and now could speak, bound and now free. The text reveals that he was brought to Jesus, but it does not say who brought him. This shows that someone believed in Jesus' power to deliver and had mercy on that man.

A key teaching from this story is that we already have enough signs to believe in Jesus. He doesn't need to prove Himself anymore; He already did so by dying on the cross for us, by conquering death and hell, and by rising again. He already overcame. Many times, things in our lives happen differently than we expect, but we need to remember that despite the circumstances, God is still God.

That man was imprisoned, mute and blind, but received back his voice, freedom and sight through the miracle—unlike the Pharisees, who were spiritually blind and, even after witnessing the miracle, still could not see Jesus as the promised Messiah.

What stood out to you the most?

_____

_____

_____

_____

_____

How can this reflection enhance your spiritual life?

_____

_____

_____

_____

_____

What would you say to Jesus today?

_____

_____

_____

_____

_____

"What then shall we say to these things? If God is for us, who can be against us? He who did not spare His own Son, but delivered Him up for us all, how shall He not with Him also freely give us all things? Who shall bring a charge against God's elect? It is God who justifies."

Romans 8:31-33

THE CRIPPLED WOMAN

For years, she saw only the ground, lost in her pain and limitations. The weight of illness stole her dreams and hope. One day, the divine gaze found her, and healing came, lifting her from humiliation to the fullness of life.

On a Saturday, Jesus was teaching in a synagogue. A woman who had been sick for eighteen years, because of an evil spirit. She was bent over and could not straighten up. When Jesus saw her, He called her and said:
— Woman, you are healed. He laid His hands on her, and she immediately straightened up and began to praise God. But the synagogue leader was indignant because Jesus had healed on the Sabbath. So he said to the people:
— There are six days for work. Come and be healed on those days, but not on the Sabbath! Then the Lord answered:
— Hypocrites! Doesn't each of you on the Sabbath untie his ox or donkey from the stall and lead it out to give it water? And this woman, a daughter of Abraham, whom Satan has kept bound for eighteen long years, should she not be set free on the Sabbath day from what bound her? When He said this, all His opponents were humiliated, but the people were delighted with all the wonderful things He was doing. Luke 13:10-16

For eighteen years, that woman's illness imprisoned her, but when Jesus saw her, He called her and quickly healed her. What took many years without Jesus was resolved in just a moment with Him.

The sickness of this woman had specific details that make her unique among Jesus' miracles. She could see, but because she was bent over, she could only look at the ground. It was much easier for her to see the soil than to lift her eyes to the sky. Surely, she knew every hole, every stone, and every doorstep of the village streets. She knew who swept the sidewalks properly and who left trash on the street. If she was walking with someone distracted, looking up, admiring the birds or the sky, she would quickly warn: "Watch out, there's a hole or a stone in the way!" because she was always with her eyes fixed on the ground.

This miracle probably took place in the second year of Jesus' ministry. At that time, Jesus was around thirty-two years old. If we subtract eighteen from thirty-two, we see that when this woman was imprisoned by Satan, Jesus was about fourteen or fifteen years old. Therefore, she had to wait eighteen years until Jesus was ready to heal her. This shows us that there was a time of preparation and a necessary wait until the right moment for Jesus to act.

Many people are waiting for miracles but still don't know Jesus. They wait for us to raise resources, prepare workers, and send missionaries so that they can finally receive the word of salvation and be healed. How many people around the world desperately need a miracle but have not yet encountered Jesus?

Perhaps that woman had already heard of Jesus and, because of that, went to the synagogue on that Saturday, knowing He would be there. We cannot say for sure, but one thing is clear: she was in the right place that day. Even though she was sick, oppressed, and had difficulty walking, she certainly made a great effort to get there. This shows us that every miracle requires some kind of dedication on our part. However, when she finally encountered Jesus, the miracle happened quickly and powerfully. She didn't have to wait anymore: Jesus called her and healed her immediately.

The text says: "When Jesus saw her, He called her over and said, 'Woman, you are set free from your infirmity.'" This passage also mentions that she was imprisoned by Satan. This shows us that the disease of this woman had a spiritual cause. It wasn't something emotional or hereditary. She was a healthy person until she opened a breach, allowing Satan to enter and afflict her with sickness.

Many believe that God places diseases on people, but here Jesus affirms that it was Satan who caused that woman's illness. Throughout the New Testament, Jesus never cursed anyone with a disease. When Peter wished that fire would come down from heaven to punish people, Jesus quickly rebuked him, saying, "But He turned and rebuked them, saying, 'You do not know what manner of spirit you are of. For the Son of Man did not come to destroy men's lives but to save them.'" Luke 9:55. This clearly shows us that, if there are diseases, it is not God who brings them, but Satan. The text also teaches us who heals, who frees, and who transforms.

The woman spent eighteen years in a position of humiliation. She didn't choose to be like this; she was forced to remain looking at the ground, at the holes, at the stones, until she met Jesus. He freed her not only from her illness but also from shame, rejection, and prejudice.

It's possible that Jesus had seen her before, but it wasn't the right time. I imagine Jesus walking through the village with His mother and asking, "Mother, why is that woman bent over?" She had to wait eighteen years until Jesus began His ministry to help her.

Today, we don't have to wait to meet Jesus. He has already conquered everything we need. There is no more waiting for Him to win, because He has already won. He has given us all authority in His name to be healed from any illness. Those eighteen years were necessary, but today, grace is available, power is available, blessing is available. Faith and the certainty of victory must be in our hearts. That woman, surely, knew all the details of the road, but when she met Jesus, she began to look up and glorify God. When we are enslaved by sin, we cannot see the sky, only the difficulties and impossibilities, but when Jesus comes, He sets us free.

What stood out to you the most?

_____

_____

_____

_____

_____

How can this reflection enhance your spiritual life?

_____

_____

_____

_____

What would you say to Jesus today?

_____

_____

_____

_____

"Ask, and it will be given to you; seek, and you will find; knock, and it will be opened to you. For everyone who asks receives, and he who seeks finds, and to him who knocks, it will be opened. And who among you, if his son asks for bread, will give him a stone? Or if he asks for a fish, will give him a serpent? Now, if you, being evil, know how to give good gifts to your children, how much more will your Father in heaven give good things to those who ask Him!"
Matthew 7:7-11

THE STORM

While the sea was raging fiercely, someone slept peacefully, enjoying every second of rest. The others, tense, were already thinking about death; meanwhile, He had not a single concern.

On that day, when evening had come, He said to them, "Let us go over to the other side." And they, leaving the crowd behind, took Him along just as He was in the boat; and there were also other little boats with Him. And a great windstorm arose, and the waves were breaking over the boat, so that it was already filling with water. But He was in the stern, sleeping on a cushion; and they woke Him and said to Him, "Teacher, do You not care that we are perishing?" And He got up, rebuked the wind and said to the sea, "Peace, be still!" Then the wind ceased, and there was a great calm. And He said to them, "Why are you so afraid? Do you still have no faith?" And they were filled with great fear and said to one another, "Who then is this, that even the wind and the sea obey Him?"
Mark 4:35-41

This wasn't supposed to be a long journey, and surely the disciples knew the route well. Being local fishermen, they had certainly made that trip many times. What could go wrong? The plan was simple: "We'll leave at dusk and arrive by nightfall." The boat was ready, everyone on board, and soon they would be on the other side. However, the wind and the waters had other plans for them.

Suddenly, conditions that had been favorable turned difficult, and the journey that was supposed to be ordinary became challenging. As time passed, more problems piled up, and now water was beginning to fill the boat. The water should have stayed outside the boat, not inside—this meant that soon everyone would be in the lake, in the middle of a storm.

This miracle was different from all the previous ones, as it involved elements of nature. Perhaps the disciples had never seen Jesus perform this type of miracle before. That's why they were astonished and asked, "Who is this?" If we pay close attention, the disciples woke Jesus with a question: "Teacher, don't You care that we're perishing?" Jesus stood up, performed the miracle, and they continued questioning: "Who is this man?" The disciples' faith was constantly being tested, and many times they hesitated to ask questions because they still didn't fully understand Him.

As we reflect on this passage, we notice an important detail: there wasn't just one boat in that storm. If we go back to the text, we read: "They took Him along, just as He was, in the boat and other boats were with Him." Who was in those other boats? Certainly, people who followed Jesus wherever He went.

When Jesus' fame spread, He had to retreat to isolated places because crowds would pack the towns He visited. Sometimes, He preached from a boat to avoid being crushed by the crowd. So when He crossed to the other side, people with boats followed Him. The text doesn't tell us what happened to those other boats in the storm. Did they perish?

The disciples were experienced fishermen, familiar with the lake and skilled in navigating the boat. They waited until the very last moment to call on Jesus—when there was nothing else they could do. Let's go back to the initial question: what about the other boats?

Those other boats didn't have Jesus with them, and that's striking. Many times, people want to follow Jesus from afar, without true commitment. They say things like: "I know Jesus, I go to church occasionally. My mother was a Christian, my father too..." Yet they are not in the boat with Jesus. They're just following from a distance. That's dangerous!

Now, if even those who were with Jesus felt the waves, the wind, and the rocking of the boat, imagine facing a storm without Him? Who is with us during our difficulties makes all the difference! Going through a storm without God is too risky. You might not make it without Jesus' help.

When Jesus declared, "Let us go over to the other side," He took responsibility for that journey—even choosing to rest, preparing for what they would do on the other side. Faith rests. It doesn't fear, rush, or despair. We need to remember that if Jesus made a promise, He will fulfill it!

If the disciples had remembered those words and known who Jesus was, they could have said to one another: "It's impossible for this boat to sink, because Jesus, the Son of God, is with us." When we believe that the Son of God is with us and that His Spirit dwells in us, our faith begins to see our victory. If Jesus promised you something, trust Him! He will fulfill it!

Even if storms, difficulties, and trials come, Jesus warned us: "In this world you will have trouble. However, take heart! I have overcome the world!" John 16:32.

When the storm comes and you think you're going to perish, Jesus stands up and says: "Quiet, be still!" That's the difference for those who are in the right place. Everyone will face hardships, but only those who are with God will see the storm disappear. Who is this, that even the wind and the sea obey Him? He is Jesus, the Son of God, our Savior! He left His glory to die for us, so that we could make it to the other side.

The other side: eternity. There is an eternity with God and an eternity without God. Eternity with God is only possible if Jesus is in your heart! Believe in the Word of God! If you believe, Jesus will speak to your storm: "Quiet, be still!"

What stood out to you the most?

_____

_____

_____

_____

_____

How can this reflection enhance your spiritual life?

_____

_____

_____

_____

What would you say to Jesus today?

_____

_____

_____

_____

_____

"Behold, the hour is coming, and has now come, when you will
be scattered, each to his own, and will leave me alone. Yet I am
not alone, because the Father is with me. I have told you these
things so that in me you may have peace; in the world you will
have tribulation. But take heart; I have overcome the world."
John 16:32-33

77

THE GADARENE

He spent his days and nights in the tombs, wandering aimlessly, prisoner of an invisible burden. He walked everywhere, but he was not free. Even shackled, he walked, for his chains could not hold him, but the spiritual prison weighed on his soul like shadows that never dissipated.

They sailed to the region of the Gadarenes, which is opposite to Galilee. When Jesus stepped ashore, a man from the town met Him. This man had been possessed by demons for a long time. He was not wearing clothes, and he did not live in a house but in the tombs. Even chains could not bind him, for he had often been chained hand and foot, but he tore the chains apart and broke the irons on his feet. No one was strong enough to subdue him.

Night and day, among the tombs and in the hills, he would cry out and cut himself with stones. When he saw Jesus from a distance, he ran and fell on his knees in front of Him. He shouted at the top of his voice, "What do you want with me, Jesus, Son of the Most High God? In God's name, don't torture me!" For Jesus had said to him, "Come out of this man, you impure spirit!"

Then Jesus asked him, "What is your name?" "My name is Legion," he replied, "for we are many." And he begged Jesus again and again not to send them out of the area.

A large herd of pigs was feeding on the nearby hillside. The demons begged Jesus, "Send us among the pigs; allow us to go into them." He gave them permission, and the impure spirits came out and went into the pigs. The herd, about two thousand in number, rushed down the steep bank into the lake and were drowned.

Those tending the pigs ran off and reported this in the town and countryside, and the people went out to see what had happened. When they came to Jesus, they found the man who had

78

been possessed by the legion of demons sitting there, dressed and in his right mind; and they were afraid.

Those who had seen it told the people what had happened to the demon-possessed man and told about the pigs as well. Then the people began to plead with Jesus to leave their region.

As Jesus was getting into the boat, the man who had been demon-possessed begged to go with Him. Jesus did not let him, but said, "Go home to your own people and tell them how much the Lord has done for you, and how He has had mercy on you." So the man went away and began to tell in the Decapolis how much Jesus had done for him. And all the people were amazed. Luke 8:26 and Mark 5:3

The land of the Gadarenes was part of the Decapolis, a group of ten cities with Greek influence located to the east of the Jordan River. This region was culturally different from the rest of Palestine, as its population was predominantly Gentile. This explains the presence of pigs, which are unclean animals according to the Jewish law in Leviticus 11:7. The demon-possessed man lived in isolation, outside the city, dwelling among the tombs, a common practice among the marginalized of that time. He was a threat to society, unable to be contained, and represented the destructive impact of demonic oppression.

This miracle is rich in details, and unlike others, it is a lengthy account. For this reason, I decided to combine the passages from Mark and Luke to tell this story. There were two demon-possessed men mentioned in Matthew's account, but only one interacted with Jesus, and it is about him that we will reflect.

We realize that there is no one so terrible, so difficult, or so despicable that Jesus cannot save. Jesus made a boat trip with His disciples to reach these men. They were the only people Jesus saved in that land, and this shows that He does not prioritize anyone based on categories or conditions. He always went where there was someone in need of a miracle or salvation.

It is hard to compare the suffering of this man with that of others who received miracles, but without a doubt, he is among those who could most certainly say: "I was exceedingly blessed by God." He was rejected, excluded from society, despised, hated, forgotten, tormented, enslaved, and disqualified. He was discarded by the city and feared by all. To his family and to society, he was like a living dead. He did not socialize because he was dominated by violent spirits that tormented him. For this reason, he lived among the mountains and the graves, where he cut himself. His pain was not only emotional and spiritual but also physical.

Looking at his story, I realize that he could not have sunk any deeper. In every aspect—physical, mental, and spiritual—he was a tormented man. Even so, Jesus came to set him free, and when it was all over, he wanted to follow Jesus. He was told to return to his family and testify about the wonders God had done in his life.

Many of us who hear this reflection need to do the same: go out and tell others about the wonders God has done in our lives. The greatest of them all is the deliverance from sin. We are no longer slaves but free in Christ Jesus. Yet, we keep our stories and testimonies. For what? For whom? How many people are enslaved and tormented today? How many are marginalized because of the curses in their lives? The only thing they need to hear is that there is hope, that there is a Savior, someone who can deliver and give a new life.

There is a saying that goes: "A soul is worth more than the whole world." Although it is not a verse, it is a biblical truth. Matthew 16:26 says: "For what will it profit a man if he gains the whole world, and forfeits his soul? Or what will a man give in exchange for his soul?" This means that nothing in the world compares to salvation. This is why Jesus went to the land of the Gadarenes to rescue that man who was enslaved. In Romans 1:16, it says: "For I am not ashamed of the gospel, because it is the power of God that brings salvation to everyone who believes." I am sure that the Gadarene was not ashamed of the miracle he received. He went throughout the Decapolis telling his testimony.

The account of the demon-possessed Gadarene is one of the most impressive miracles of Jesus and reveals His absolute power over spiritual forces. This miracle teaches us about deliverance, transformation, and mission. The encounter between Jesus and this tormented man shows that no one is beyond the reach of God's grace. As we analyze this passage, we will see its impact not only on the life of the Gadarene but also on the society around him.

The encounter between Jesus and the Gadarene demonstrates divine authority over the kingdom of darkness. Upon seeing Jesus, the possessed man recognizes His identity and falls before Him. The demonic legion begs not to be cast out of the region and requests to enter the pigs, which then rush into the sea. The miracle shocks the locals, who, instead of glorifying God, ask Jesus to leave. The Gadarene, now freed and in his right mind, wants to follow Jesus but is given a mission: to testify in his homeland.

Jesus has absolute power to deliver anyone. The Gadarene was in a condition of total destruction, but he was completely restored. This teaches us that no matter how deep the spiritual oppression, Jesus has the authority to transform any life.

The reaction of the people to the Gadarene's deliverance warns us about resistance to the work of God. The locals were more concerned about the material loss of the pigs than the liberation of a man. This shows that not everyone values spiritual things, and we must be prepared for rejection as we testify about Christ.

Every saved person has a mission to fulfill. The Gadarene wanted to follow Jesus, but he was told to return home and tell what God had done. Just like him, we are called to testify about the transforming power of Christ, bringing the message of deliverance to those still living in darkness.

What stood out to you the most?

_____

_____

_____

_____

_____

How can this reflection enhance your spiritual life?

_____

_____

_____

_____

_____

_____

What would you say to Jesus today?

_____

_____

_____

_____

_____

_____

*"For I will be merciful to their unrighteousness, and their sins
and their lawless deeds I will remember no more."*
Hebrews 8:12

THE WOMAN WITH THE BLOOD ISSUE

"Today is the day of my miracle!" she thought. "I just need to touch him, because when I do, I will be healed!" That was her motivation: a goal, a target, a purpose, because miracles come from heaven, but they don't fall out of nowhere.

A great multitude followed Him and pressed around Him. And a certain woman, who had had a flow of blood for twelve years, and had suffered much under many physicians, and had spent all that she had, and was no better but rather grew worse, when she heard about Jesus, came up behind Him in the crowd and touched His garment. For she said, "If I can just touch His clothes, I will be healed." Immediately the fountain of her blood was dried up, and she felt in her body that she was healed of her affliction. And immediately Jesus, knowing in Himself that power had gone out from Him, turned around in the crowd and said, "Who touched My clothes?" And His disciples said to Him, "You see the multitude pressing against You, and You say, 'Who touched Me?'" And He looked around to see who had done this. Then the woman, knowing what had happened to her, came in fear and trembling, fell down before Him and told Him the whole truth. And He said to her, "Daughter, your faith has saved you. Go in peace and be healed of your affliction." Mark 5:24b–34

The miracle of the woman with the issue of blood happened at a time when, according to the law, women could not touch anyone while bleeding. If this happened, they had to remain isolated for seven days. That was the established precept. That's why, when she touched Jesus, she was afraid, for she could be accused of breaking the law. Yet she faced her fear, moved forward, and touched Him, believing in the miracle.

Looking at this miracle, I notice that many were touching Jesus but didn't receive their miracles. The woman, however, touched Him with faith and was healed, while others, even though close to Him, received nothing. This is remarkable, because the crowd pressed around Him, but only she, with faith, experienced the power of healing and obtained what she sought.

Another important point is that the text says: "when she heard about Jesus." Isn't this exactly what the Word teaches us? That faith comes by hearing? How many miracles have happened because people heard about Jesus and decided to believe? That woman heard and believed, while others didn't. She touched with faith, while others didn't, and that's why she received healing, while others received nothing.

In another passage, in Matthew 9:21, we see her declaration of faith: "For she said within herself, If I may but touch his garment, I shall be whole." She declared, even before receiving the miracle, that she had already claimed it. I believe that, many times, indignation drives us to reach what we would not otherwise have the strength to conquer. When we reach the point of indignation, we decide to take hold of what belongs to us. That woman, when she touched Jesus, was not just waiting for a miracle. She was declaring she would receive it.

When the miracle happened, Jesus realized someone had touched Him in a different way. In the previous reflection, we spoke about the man from Gadara, for whom Jesus crossed the sea and went to his land to rescue him. In the woman's case, it was she who went to Jesus in search of her miracle. That makes me think: while Jesus offers us salvation, our miracle requires that we walk in faith.

We should not just wait for Jesus to come to us so we can receive Him. He offers us salvation, the Word, and the freedom to pursue our miracle. Money did not solve that woman's problem. Neither did science. Nor did time. Today, with money, it's possible to solve many problems, and science offers solutions to various diseases. Some say "time heals everything," but time did not heal her. Twelve years passed, and time was not able to cure her. What problem have you been facing for years that time has not solved? What challenge can't money fix? Or science? This woman proved that even with money, science, and time on her side, only Jesus could do what none of these could.

She didn't know Jesus until then, but when she heard the Word, something inside her changed. The Word transformed her life from the inside out, and that led her to declare: "I will receive my miracle." She heard about Jesus, believed, and acted. She went after Jesus, not waiting passively for the healing to come to her. If you hear the Word of God and believe, it will change you from within and begin to bear fruit until, finally, you declare: "I will receive my miracle, because my God is good and He is powerful to heal, save, and transform." That was the case for the woman, and it can be yours too, because Jesus is the same yesterday, today, and forever.

Before, she was known as the woman who couldn't go to the temple because she was "unclean" under the Mosaic law. Twelve years away from the religious celebrations of her people, but now she was called blessed, because she had been healed by the prophet. Isolated from everyone, she couldn't visit the homes of her friends. How many births, baptisms, and weddings did she miss? I believe many. Now, everyone wanted her to visit and tell the story of her miracle. People wanted to know what it was like to receive a healing of that magnitude and probably asked her, "What else did Jesus say to you?" Surely, she answered, "Daughter, your faith has saved you; go in peace!" Jesus gave that woman something she likely hadn't had in many years: peace! If the Lord had not healed her, just having God's peace would have been worth it. Nevertheless, that peace came with a great blessing.

Finally, the one who had been isolated from those she loved could now be embraced again by her family. So much affection, once withheld, could now be restored in her new condition of wholeness. From isolated to welcomed, from rejected to recognized, from cursed to blessed. This was the story of the woman who did not give up on her miracle.

What stood out to you the most?

_____

_____

_____

_____

_____

How can this reflection enhance your spiritual life?

_____

_____

_____

_____

_____

What would you say to Jesus today?

_____

_____

_____

_____

_____

_____

*"If you abide in Me, and My words abide in you, you
will ask what you desire, and it shall be done for you."*
John 15:7

JAIRUS' DAUGHTER

Time was his greatest enemy, and with each passing moment, fear took over. Bad news spread faster than he could keep up with, and the miracle seemed farther and farther away. His heart raced until he found the one he was seeking, and then he fell to the ground, without shame or restraint. It all seemed impossible and out of reach—until the Author of life said to him, "Do not be afraid!"

When Jesus crossed over again by boat to the other side, a great crowd gathered around Him, and He was by the sea. Then one of the leaders of the synagogue, named Jairus, came, and when he saw Him, he fell at His feet and pleaded with Him earnestly, saying, "My daughter is dying. I beg You, come and lay Your hands on her so that she may be healed and live." So He went with him, and a large crowd followed Him and pressed around Him.

While He was still speaking, some people came from the house of the synagogue leader, saying, "Your daughter is dead. Why trouble the Master any longer?" But Jesus, overhearing what was said, said to the synagogue leader, "Do not be afraid, only believe." And He did not allow anyone to follow Him except Peter, James, and John, the brother of James. When they came to the house of the synagogue leader, He saw a commotion, with people crying and wailing loudly. He went in and said to them, "Why are you making such a commotion and crying? The girl is not dead but asleep." And they laughed at Him. But He put them all outside, took the child's father and mother and those who were with Him, and went in where the child was. Taking her by the hand, He said to her, "Talitha cumi," which means, "Little girl, I say to you, get up." Immediately the girl got up and began to walk around—she was twelve years old. At this, they were completely astonished. And He strictly ordered them that no one should know about this, and told them to give her something to eat. Luke 8:40–56

Who was Jairus? Jairus was the leader of the synagogue. In Jesus' time, a leader of the synagogue was a Pharisee well-versed in the law and its interpretation. He oversaw the functioning of the synagogue, the prayers, and the entire organization of that place of worship. We see Jairus as a desperate man, for the text says he threw himself at Jesus' feet. Many times Jesus criticized the Pharisees for their rigidity in following the law, for their hypocrisy, and for many other behaviors that caused them to dislike him. Many Pharisees plotted Jesus' death and hated him because he confronted not the law itself, but the way they followed it. For a synagogue leader to throw himself at Jesus' feet, it was necessary to acknowledge that all his knowledge, status, and position no longer served any purpose. At that moment, the most important thing for that man was Jesus' mercy.

The miracle of Jairus' daughter is presented alongside the miracle of the woman with the issue of blood. The previous text tells us that story. When Jairus asked Jesus to go to his house to see his daughter, Jesus agreed and began walking there. However, at that moment, the woman with the issue of blood appeared and interrupted the journey.

We can imagine Jairus watching the whole situation, which only delayed Jesus' arrival at his house. Jesus was on his way to his house and, suddenly, had to stop to talk to the woman who had touched him and been healed. Surely, Jairus already knew the story of that woman, as she had probably sought help at the synagogue several times, asking for prayers. Everyone knew who she was. That woman delayed Jairus' miracle. However, we notice some important characteristics in her behavior. He was humble, had faith, and patience to wait for Jesus. When the people arrived and told him, "Your daughter is already dead, do not trouble the Teacher anymore," Jesus answered, "Do not be afraid, only believe." At that moment, Jairus chose to obey.

This man had all the prerequisites to receive a miracle. He took action, had faith because he knew that if Jesus laid his hands on his daughter, she would be healed. However, before the miracle happened, he had to face challenges. He had to deal with his reputation, which was tainted by seeking the help of someone the Pharisees rejected.

He had humility and patience to wait. If he hadn't had patience, he wouldn't have received the miracle. When those men said that his daughter had died, that was the perfect moment to give up. Sometimes we are near a miracle when someone comes and tells us that what we want is impossible. What they told Jairus was not a lie. Indeed, his daughter had died. What the natural man cannot see is the impossible being turned into a possibility by God. When those men said, "Do not trouble the Teacher anymore," it was like a bad diagnosis, a negative result, a shattered dream.

For us, almost everything is impossible, and if it weren't for God in our lives, even breathing would be impossible. It is not by the strength of our arm that we conquer our victories, but by God's power, who gives us wisdom, intelligence, health, and gifts. Jairus could have become upset with the woman who had the issue of blood and blamed the delay for his daughter's death. However, he did not act that way; he focused on Jesus' word: "Do not be afraid, only believe."

When they arrived at Jairus' house, the environment was not conducive to a miracle. Everyone was crying and mourning, so Jesus removed those people. There are moments when we need to remove everything that brings us down—people who speak negative words, who remind us of the past, of failures, of impossibilities. All these voices need to be removed from our lives, as Jesus did by removing the unbelievers from the house.

Could Jesus have healed the girl without doing this? Yes, but He did it because it was the best thing. When He removed all that negativity, He helped the parents continue believing. We should also do the same with memories and negative feelings that hinder us. We need to focus on God's word, on what He says about our life, on what He affirms that we are and can achieve.

Jairus had many opportunities to fail in his faith, but he gave us great examples of perseverance. At first, he believed that Jesus needed to lay hands on his daughter for her to be healed. However, after witnessing the miracle of the woman with the issue of blood, he had to decide. Would he believe the word of the people who said there was no more solution, or would he believe Jesus' word, which said, "Do not be afraid, only believe"? The question is: whom will you believe? Will you believe the voices that say you cannot, you are not able, and you will not succeed? Or will you trust in Jesus, who says that everything is possible for those who believe?

The miracle in Jairus' life was great, and the testimony even greater. To receive a miracle, we need to let go of many things, abandon concepts and baggage, and simply believe in God's word. After that, we do not need to do anything else. That girl "slept" a sleep that few desire to sleep, but her father was working for her. She did not know or perceive what was happening around her, while he ran from side to side to give her back life. He did not rest or delegate that mission to anyone else until he saw his beloved daughter alive again. Isn't that how God works with us? While we sleep tired, the Lord works tirelessly to give us hope and a future. We can't even imagine how, but God always works in our favor.

If we were to seek a key lesson from this miracle, it would be this: the final word in our lives will always come from the Lord. The last word of our story comes from God, for He can change any situation. They told Jairus that his daughter was dead, but God brought the final word: "*Do not be afraid, only believe!*"

What stood out to you the most?

_____

_____

_____

_____

_____

How can this reflection enhance your spiritual life?

_____

_____

_____

_____

_____

What would you say to Jesus today?

_____

_____

_____

_____

_____

"For nothing will be impossible with God!"
Luke 1:37

THE TWO BLIND MEN

Two men, blind to the world but not to hope, walked together in the darkness, guided by hope. Their hearts saw the impossible, and their voices cried out for mercy. In their encounter with Jesus, not only were their eyes opened, but their souls were reborn to eternal light. They were companions in suffering, but also in redemption.

Jesus left that place, and on the way, two blind men began to follow Him, shouting:
— Son of David, have mercy on us!
As soon as Jesus entered the house, the blind men came to Him. Then He asked them:
— Do you believe that I can heal you?
— Yes, Lord! We believe! — they answered Him.
Jesus touched their eyes and said:
— Let it be done for you according to your faith!
And their eyes were healed. Then Jesus sternly warned them:
— Do not tell anyone about this!
But they went out and spread the news about Him throughout that region. Matthew 9:27-31

Jesus, in some situations, asked people not to openly share the miracles, because whenever that happened, His fame grew greatly, making it difficult for Him to enter the cities. However, these two blind men couldn't keep the secret. We've seen on other occasions that Jesus asked people not to share the miracles, but many couldn't obey. It is understandable, as a miracle of such magnitude is hard to hide.

They cried out: "Son of David, have mercy on us!" Those men shouted as if they had received the revelation of Jesus' messianic title. This messianic title acknowledges Jesus as the promised descendant of David, who would bring deliverance (II Samuel 7:12-16; Isaiah 11:1-5).

"Do you believe that I can heal you?" Jesus asked them to make them declare their faith. They needed to confess their belief so that their faith would be revealed to everyone and to themselves as well. Only after they confessed their faith did the miracle happen, and Jesus said: "Let it be done for you according to your faith!" This reveals the dynamic of this miracle. They believed, confessed, and received. We will see this same dynamic in many miracles. Jesus often used His faith and authority to deliver demon-possessed and sick people who couldn't hear or speak, but whenever He encountered faith, He declared, "Your faith has healed or saved you."

The text tells us that the blind men followed Jesus, found Him, and entered the house where He was. However, how could a blind man find something? This makes me understand that they were led by someone. These anonymous people may be the most important part of this miracle, for without them, those blind men would have never found Jesus. They would never have entered the house where He was if no one had guided them.

I see this as a great lesson for today. If we don't lead people to Jesus, if we don't talk about Him, many will remain spiritually blind. There is a generation of blind people searching for a way out, but unable to find salvation and we, as knowers of the Word, often fail to bring spiritual blind people to an encounter with Jesus.

Jesus is ready and waiting. He said, "Where two or three are gathered in My name, there I am in the midst of them." Therefore, every church that preaches the genuine Gospel has the presence of Jesus. However, it is our responsibility to bring these spiritually blind people to know the Word of Salvation and be set free.

Many have heard of Jesus, say they believe in Him, but have never had a real encounter with Him. Ask a person: "Do you believe in God?" They may answer yes. But if you ask: "Have you had an encounter with Jesus? Have you given your life to Him?"

many will say no. This shows our failure in communicating the Kingdom.

How many people have we failed to invite to hear the salvation message? I remember when I was preparing for college entrance exams. There was a classmate who always arrived late. I sat at the back of the room and always saved a seat for him. We became friends and talked about Jesus. He had many doubts and was thirsty for answers. One day, I invited him to go to church. On his first visit, he just listened, but on the second, he accepted Jesus. To this day, he stands firm, sharing the good news of salvation with his family. If I hadn't extended that invitation, maybe my words wouldn't have been enough to help him. After all, it is the Holy Spirit who convinces man of sin, righteousness, and judgment.

If those people hadn't brought the blind men to Jesus, they would never have been healed. Guiding a blind person isn't easy; it requires paying attention to the path, holding their hand, observing obstacles along the way, and it demands effort, time, and dedication. I am sure that those who led them were rewarded with their healing and the spreading of God's glory in that city. Even though Jesus told them not to openly speak about it, they couldn't hide the miracle. The glory was so great they needed to announce it.

How will people find Jesus if there is no one to preach, teach, and lead them to His presence? We need to preach Jesus, the author and finisher of our faith, the one who performs miracles, heals, transforms lives, and gives us the assurance of eternal life.

This miracle shows us the importance of those who led the blind men to Jesus. These people don't appear in the text, but without them, the miracle wouldn't have happened. Be that anonymous person, an instrument in the Lord's hands, to lead people to the marvelous grace of Jesus.

What stood out to you the most?

_____

_____

_____

_____

_____

How can this reflection enhance your spiritual life?

_____

_____

_____

_____

_____

What would you say to Jesus today?

_____

_____

_____

_____

_____

"Truly, truly I say to you, whoever believes in Me will also do the works that I do; and greater works than these will he do, because I am going to the Father."
John 14:12

THE MUTE MAN OF CAPERNAUM

He could not speak, but he heard the world around him. His lips longed to scream, yet he remained imprisoned. His cell had no iron bars or concrete walls; it was made of silence, and within it lived his torment.

Then they went away and spread the news about Jesus throughout that entire region. When they had left, some people brought to Jesus a man who could not speak because he was possessed by a demon. As soon as the demon was cast out, the man began to speak. Everyone was amazed and said:
— We have never seen anything like this in Israel!
But the Pharisees said:
— It is the ruler of the demons who gives this man power to cast out demons.
Jesus went around visiting all the towns and villages. He taught in the synagogues, proclaimed the good news about the Kingdom, and healed all kinds of sicknesses and serious diseases among the people. When Jesus saw the crowd, he was filled with deep compassion for them because they were distressed and helpless, like sheep without a shepherd. Then he said to his disciples:
— The harvest is truly great, but the workers are few. Ask the Lord of the harvest to send more workers to gather in the harvest.
Matthew 9:31-38

This miracle is part of a series of healings and deliverances that Jesus performed in that region, demonstrating His compassion for the suffering and His authority over evil. He not only healed physical illnesses but also set people free from spiritual oppression. This episode also foreshadows the growing conflict between Jesus and the religious leaders of the time, who refused to acknowledge His divine authority.

We know little about this man. We don't know his name, who he was, what he did, or how long he had been imprisoned in that condition. He was most likely a simple man, without any social prominence. Because of his condition, he was perhaps known as "the mute possessed man." People recognized him for his situation and no longer for who he truly was. His identity had been altered by that demonic spirit.

His condition was terrible because he couldn't ask for help. He was like someone who falls into a deep pit and has no voice to cry out for rescue. Even without speaking, Jesus heard his soul crying for help. However, he had something in his favor: the people who brought him to Jesus. Without these people, Jesus wouldn't have performed this miracle. In the same way, if we don't come to Jesus with our problems and petitions, He won't perform miracles in our lives.

This miracle was just one among many that day, but what caught the writer's attention was the context surrounding the event. The text doesn't describe the man's interaction with Jesus; it simply says he was delivered and began to speak. However, we will find five characters involved in this moment: the man's friends, the amazed crowd, the Pharisees, Jesus, and the man who was set free. Each of these characters shows a different aspect of the miracle.

The friends believed in Jesus' power and decided to help the man, hoping to see him delivered from that evil. Who were these people? Friends, acquaintances, or family members? We'll never know, but one thing is certain: they decided to face the opposition of the religious leaders who were already beginning to persecute Jesus. Their attitude is commendable because they left their own responsibilities to help someone who could not repay them. This was a true display of altruism.

The crowd was amazed because they had never seen anything like it in Israel. They had never witnessed such miracles, though they had heard about Jesus. That was the reason why multitudes followed Him wherever He went. The people's admiration for Jesus' miracles made the Pharisees see Him as a threat to their religious authority over the people. With each passing day, the crowd grew larger, and so did the opposition from the religious leadership.

The Pharisees were an influential religious and political group in first-century Judaism. They were known for their strict observance of the Law of Moses and oral traditions. Despite being religious and obedient to commandments, they had no compassion for the sick. Instead of rejoicing over the man's deliverance, they criticized and accused Jesus of being a fraud.

The man who came oppressed and silenced by evil behaved differently. What he couldn't do before, he was now able to do. His voice could now reach everyone around him. Perhaps he didn't even understand what was happening, but now he was free. With just one encounter with Jesus, his life was completely transformed. The people who had known him as "the mute possessed man" would now have to call him by his name, no longer by his past condition.

We will often see that some people were healed and delivered purely by the Lord's mercy. These people did not display any faith or desire, but God's grace reached them anyway. In the same way, we receive our salvation. We did nothing to earn it, we didn't even seek it, and we certainly didn't deserve it, but God granted it to us nonetheless. We didn't know salvation and, when we finally understood it, we realized we were separated from the glory of God. However, because of His infinite love and mercy, He gave us the opportunity to receive eternal life through His Son.

An encounter with Jesus is all we need for our lives to be completely changed, like a true miracle. In fact, this miracle will happen if you believe that He has the power to heal, deliver, and restore your life.

What stood out to you the most?

_____

_____

_____

_____

How can this reflection enhance your spiritual life?

_____

_____

_____

_____

_____

What would you say to Jesus today?

_____

_____

_____

_____

_____

_____

*"so that you may comprehend, with all the saints, what is the
width and length and depth and height; and to know the love of
Christ, which surpasses understanding; that you may be filled
with all the fullness of God. Now to Him who is able to do far
more abundantly than all we ask or think, according
to the power that works in us"*
Ephesians 3:18-20

THE FIRST MULTIPLICATION

They had heard about Him, and hope grew in their hearts. Many had witnessed miracles and signs. He was in the wilderness and to the wilderness they went; carrying pain, longings, and the thirst for a touch that would restore their lives.

Now the Passover, the feast of the Jews, was near, and they went away in a boat to a deserted place by themselves. But the crowds saw them going and many recognized Him. Then they ran on foot from all the towns, arrived before them, and came near Him. When Jesus got out of the boat, He saw a large crowd and had compassion on them, because they were like sheep without a shepherd.

So He began to teach them many things. When it was already late, His disciples came to Him and said: "This place is deserted, and the hour is already late. Send them away so they may go into the surrounding fields and villages and buy themselves some bread, for they have nothing to eat." But He answered: "You give them something to eat."

They replied: "Shall we go and buy two hundred denarii worth of bread to give them to eat?" Then He said to them: "How many loaves do you have?" One of His disciples, Andrew, Simon Peter's brother, said to Him: "There is a boy here who has five barley loaves and two small fish, but what are these for so many?"

He commanded them to make everyone sit down in groups on the green grass. And they sat down in groups of hundreds and fifties. He took the five loaves and the two fish, looked up to heaven, blessed them, broke the loaves, and gave them to His disciples to set before the people. He also divided the two fish among them all. Everyone ate and was satisfied. And they picked up twelve baskets full of broken pieces of bread and fish. Those who ate the loaves were about five thousand men. John 6:4, Mark 6:32

Wherever Jesus went, the crowds followed Him. When they heard He would be in that place, the news spread, and everyone ran to Bethsaida, near the Sea of Galilee, arriving even before Him. The text says Jesus had compassion on those people, for they were lost, without knowledge, like sheep without a shepherd. They were spiritually wandering, not knowing where they came from or where they were going.

Jesus then began to teach, and the entire day passed that way. Luke, in his account, adds: "and spoke to them about the Kingdom of God and healed those who needed healing." In other miracles, we see that the crowds stayed with Him for days, listening to His word. In this one, it happened in a single day, for the text says it was already late. The disciples brought up the issue of the people's food, but Jesus had already noticed it, as we read in John 6:5: "Jesus looked up and saw a great crowd coming toward Him. He said to Philip, 'Where shall we buy bread for these people to eat?' He knew very well what He was going to do, but He asked this to test Philip."

We can imagine the details surrounding this miracle: how it happened and how it led to the final outcome. Maybe a boy was at home, heard the commotion, asked what was going on, and found out that the prophet Jesus was nearby. He wanted to go see Him, but his mother, like a typical Jewish mother, wouldn't let him go without food. So she prepared some loaves and fish for him. The boy put everything in his small sheep-leather pouch and went toward the crowd.

If he had known what would happen with those loaves and fish, perhaps he would have said to the other kids: "I'm taking food for this whole crowd!" In truth, he was carrying the seed of a great miracle. What's interesting is that he was alone. If he had been with his parents, maybe they would have given the food to Jesus, but the boy did it voluntarily. That's surprising, because many children don't share their food.

The loaves and fish weren't enough to feed that multitude. Nevertheless, Jesus doesn't need our help to perform a miracle;

He only needs our willingness and faith. The miracle is His work. Before multiplying the food, Jesus organized the crowd into groups of one hundred and fifty. This shows that He first brings order before acting. Then He had them all sit down. This was a sign for them to trust Him.

Jesus could have simply multiplied the loaves and fish and told them to be distributed, but He didn't. He chose to organize and make everyone wait. Perhaps He looked up to heaven, as usual, and blessed the food. Then everyone ate and was satisfied. What's striking is that, in the end, twelve baskets were left over. Where there was lack, there was now abundance. Where there had been doubt, there was now certainty. When God performs a miracle, He doesn't only reach you, but also your family, your friends, your coworkers, and gives us a testimony so we can glorify His name.

Now reflect: that mother, when she prepared the food, had no idea she was feeding a multitude. She simply wanted to take care of her son, but God used that act of love to feed many. The boy was probably poor, as barley was the cheapest grain, used to feed animals. Wheat was a more valuable flour, more suited for bread. He gave five loaves and two fish, but I'm sure that, in the end, he ate as many loaves and fish as he wanted.

I imagine that maybe one of the disciples gave him a large portion of loaves and fish, and as he returned home and called his mother, he said: "Mom, come see this. You know that food you made for me? It fed a crowd!" I believe that among that great multitude, other people may have brought some food, but the boy, who wasn't even counted among the five thousand, the poor and solitary one, had two qualities no one else had: he was close to Jesus and gave the best he had to the Lord.

How surprised that boy must have been to see his lunch being multiplied right before his eyes! The more he looked, the more loaves and fish multiplied. That tells me that when we are close to Jesus, suddenly a miracle can happen. When we offer our best, He will multiply it. If he hadn't offered what he had, the miracle might still have happened, but not in that way.

The disciples didn't know and couldn't imagine how it would be possible to feed that crowd, but when everything was done, twelve baskets were full, as if that number represented the disciples themselves or the twelve tribes of Israel. As if those loaves represented the Bread of Life – Jesus.

That day of miracles in the wilderness was special, because Jesus healed the sick, preached the kingdom, and still fed everyone. He healed the soul and fed the body. The great lesson of this miracle is that, even if it seems impossible, that doesn't invalidate God's power. The disciples said, "But what is this for so many?" Maybe you're saying to Jesus today, "Lord, this healing is impossible. This transformation is impossible. This problem has no solution," but Jesus says to you, "Give Me your best and let Me bless you."

God will use the least and the most unlikely to confound the great and the proud, so that in the end, His name may be glorified. It wasn't the boy, it wasn't the loaves, nor even the fish, but it was the power of God that satisfied that multitude. The Bible says that God does not show favoritism. Wherever Jesus was, He healed everyone. He desires to bless, save, and restore everyone. If the miracle is for everyone, then it is for you too.

What stood out to you the most?

_____

_____

_____

_____

_____

_____

How can this reflection enhance your spiritual life?

_____

_____

_____

_____

_____

What would you say to Jesus today?

_____

_____

_____

_____

_____

"Therefore do not be anxious, saying, 'What shall we eat?' or 'What shall we drink?' or 'What shall we wear?' For the Gentiles seek after all these things, and your heavenly Father knows that you need them all."
Matthew 6:31-32

WALKING ON WATER

The wind roared, and the waves struck even harder. In the darkness of the night, He walked over time and tides as if they were nothing. Nothing to fear, nothing to do, just returning to His own—yet His own did not recognize Him.

Immediately after, Jesus ordered the disciples to get into the boat and go ahead of Him to the west side of the lake, while He sent the people away. After sending the people away, Jesus went up a mountain to pray alone. When night came, He was there, alone. By that time the boat was already in the middle of the lake. And the waves were hitting the boat hard because the wind was blowing against it. In the early morning, between three and six o'clock, Jesus went out to them, walking on the water. When the disciples saw Jesus walking on the water, they were terrified and exclaimed:

— It's a ghost!

And they cried out in fear. At that moment Jesus said:

— Take courage! It is I! Don't be afraid!

Then Peter said:

— If it's really You, tell me to come to You on the water.

— Come! — Jesus replied.

Peter got out of the boat and began to walk on the water toward Jesus. But when he felt the strength of the wind, he became afraid and began to sink. Then he cried out:

— Lord, save me!

Immediately Jesus reached out His hand, took hold of Peter and said:

— How little faith you have! Why did you doubt?

Then the two of them got into the boat, and the wind calmed down. And the disciples worshiped Jesus, saying:

— Truly You are the Son of God! Matthew 14:22-32

This miracle could receive different titles: "Jesus Walks on the Sea," "Peter and Jesus Walk on the Water," or even "Jesus Saves Peter from Death." All would be accurate, because Peter started well but was unable to stay firm in his attempt to walk on water. Fortunately, Jesus saved him.

When Peter decided to walk on the water, he believed in a word, but he didn't have enough faith to believe he could make it all the way to Jesus. He started on impulse, but when he noticed the wind, the sea, and the darkness, fear took over and his faith began to fail. In that moment, he didn't realize that if he was already walking on the water, then the wind couldn't stop him.

The victory was already under his feet; all he needed to do was enjoy the moment. Walk to Jesus and return to the boat upon the word that sustained him. Maybe, seeing this, the other disciples would also have had the courage to get out of the boat and walk on the sea. The title of this miracle would then be: "Jesus and the Disciples Walk on the Sea." However, Peter did the only thing he couldn't do: doubt. The moment doubt arose, the word of faith that was sustaining him vanished. Faith and doubt cannot occupy the same space; where one is, the other must leave.

Jesus, on the other hand, walked on the water by faith. When Jesus walked on the sea, He didn't do so as a spirit or in a glorified body, but as a man, because He emptied Himself of His glory to come to earth and live fully as a man. The difference is that Jesus walked by faith guided by the Spirit of God, while Peter acted on impulse. In various parts of the New Testament, Peter appears impulsive, speaking and acting quickly without considering the consequences, which often leads to unwanted results.

This also happens to us when we enter into battles and storms merely on impulse, relying on our own strength but forgetting to firmly use our faith to reach victory. Suddenly, we're faced with the winds of life and feel alone, and our faith is tested. In 1 John 4:18, we read: "There is no fear in love. Nevertheless, perfect love casts out fear." If Peter had full certainty that Jesus was the Son of God and that He loved him, he would have known he would never sink. He would never have doubted.

We see that Peter was not yet fully prepared. Sometimes we are not ready either to face our challenges. We are in training and constant preparation, just like Peter during his three and a half years with Jesus. He would still be shaped to endure what was to come in his life. By the end of his journey, Peter proved that he was ready to face any challenge and even death through martyrdom, for believing in Jesus.

When Jesus entered the boat, the wind calmed down, and they all worshiped Him saying: "Truly You are the Son of God." When Jesus is with us, there is hope for rescue, and everything will calm down in the right time. Life's battles are much harder when He is not present. However, when He is in our boat, He tells us: "Be still and do not fear!" God often waits until the last moment to act. He waits until the final instant, and this tests us: Do we have faith? Are we willing to wait? God wants us to trust Him, even when the storms surround us.

Peter began to walk on the water, but he acted on impulse, without the faith necessary to reach the end. Acting on impulse never takes us to the end. To reach the finish and receive our miracle, we must believe that God loves us. Fear causes us to question God's love, but perfect love casts out all fear. What we can learn from this miracle is that doubt is the greatest enemy of our victory, and not everything that looks like faith really is. Impulse may make us take the first steps, but it's genuine faith in God, through Jesus, that elevates us. So keep believing, persevere until you receive your miracle. If you do not doubt and wait for God's timing, the victory will come when you need it most. When it comes, you will be able to say: "Lord, truly You are the Son of God."

What stood out to you the most?

_____

_____

_____

_____

How can this reflection enhance your spiritual life?

_____

_____

_____

_____

_____

What would you say to Jesus today?

_____

_____

_____

_____

_____

_____

"Love is patient, love is kind. It does not envy, it is not proud, it is not arrogant. Love does not dishonor others, it is not self-seeking, it is not easily angered, it keeps no record of wrongs. It does not delight in injustice but rejoices with the truth. It always protects, always trusts, always hopes, always perseveres. Love never fails."
1 Corinthians 13:4-8

THE CANAANITE WOMAN

How many times will I ask? If I ask many times and He hears me, what is importunity compared to salvation? My desperation pushed me, but it was His mercy that helped me. He spoke of my faith, but I was only thinking about my love. I remembered at every moment that, at home, my greatest treasure was imprisoned by evil.

Jesus went away from there and went to the region near the cities of Tyre and Sidon. A Canaanite woman, who lived in that land, came to Him and cried out:
— Lord, Son of David, have mercy on me! My daughter is severely oppressed by a demon!
But Jesus did not answer her a word. Then His disciples came to Him and urged Him, saying:
— Send her away, for she keeps crying out after us!
Jesus answered:
— I was sent only to the lost sheep of the house of Israel.
Then she came and knelt before Him, saying:
— Lord, help me!
Jesus answered:
— It is not right to take the children's bread and throw it to the little dogs.
— Yes, Lord, — she said, — but even the little dogs eat the crumbs that fall from their master's table.
— Woman, you have great faith! — Jesus replied. — Let it be done for you as you wish.
And her daughter was healed at once. When the woman returned home, she found her child lying on the bed; indeed, the demon had left her.

The Canaanites were another people, distinct from the Israelites. They inhabited the region of Canaan, which roughly corresponds to present-day Israel, Palestine, Lebanon, and parts of

Syria and Jordan. When the Israelites entered the Promised Land under Joshua's leadership, they found the Canaanites living there. The people of that woman practiced polytheistic religions, worshipping gods like Baal and Astarte, which often conflicted with the monotheistic faith of the Israelites. In Jesus' time, the term "Canaanite" was still used to refer to the descendants of these peoples, especially those living in the region of Tyre and Sidon (modern-day Lebanon), like the Canaanite woman.

The Jews considered the Canaanites as foreigners and spiritually impure. However, Jesus' encounter with the Canaanite woman demonstrates that God's salvation and grace were not limited to the Jews, but were available to all who had faith.

If a lawyer read this story, he would certainly say that this woman would make an excellent advocate. Her words and her faith were the only things she had left, and she appealed to the smallest of rights: the right to the crumbs. Jesus responded with a metaphor, comparing the Jews to the "children" and the Gentiles to the "little dogs." When Jesus used the image of the children's bread and the little dogs, He tested the woman's faith, but instead of retreating, she accepted the comparison and turned the situation in her favor. In other words, she did not argue about who deserved more but recognized that even the crumbs of God's grace would be enough for her. Her response showed humility and faith, and Jesus, seeing this, granted her request.

Intrinsically, there is an irony in this story, as the "children" did not accept Jesus in His entirety, and for that reason, the gospel spread to all the Gentile peoples. John writes in the first chapter of his book, starting at verse nine: "The true light that gives light to every man was coming into the world. He was in the world, and though the world was made through Him, the world did not recognize Him. He came to that which was His own, but His own did not receive Him."

The Canaanite woman represents all of us who, though not originally part of the chosen people, were reached by God's grace through Jesus Christ. Just as she persevered and received her blessing, we too are invited to persist in our faith, trusting that God hears and answers those who come to Him with a sincere heart.

Someone spoke of the wonders of Jesus to that woman, and from that moment on, faith and hope grew in her heart. When everything seemed lost, she remembered Jesus. When she left home, hope was in her heart. As she walked toward Jesus, she surely met people along the way who had received or heard of some miracle from the Prophet. Perhaps, with every step she took toward Him, people passing by testified to their miracles, making her faith only grow. The path that was once only of hope, now was of both hope and faith.

Which were the faster steps, the ones to Jesus or the ones back home? The steps to Jesus were painful and quick, but the steps back were filled with gratitude and peace. She left home crying for help, but returned smiling with a miracle. Jesus testified that this woman had great faith, and I believe that, if faith took her to the Lord, after receiving a word of blessing, she had no doubt that her daughter was healed.

Like the centurion's servant, this girl also received her miracle through someone who loved her. The mercy of the mother, the mercy of Jesus, and the mercy of God. There are blessings that reach us because someone decided to walk in love. People decided to love others and fight for God's grace to reach them. We were reached by God's grace and received the gospel of salvation because someone left their comfort to bring us the good news of Christ and eternal life. Jesus left heavenly life to live an earthly life, left His glory to be sacrificed for all.

What stood out to you the most?

_____

_____

_____

_____

How can this reflection enhance your spiritual life?

_____

_____

_____

_____

What would you say to Jesus today?

_____

_____

_____

_____

_____

"For with the heart one believes unto righteousness,
and with the mouth confession is made unto salvation.
For the Scripture says, 'Whoever believes in
Him will not be put to shame.'"
Romans 10:8-11

THE DEAF MAN OF DECAPOLIS

A silent day, like any other, or rather, like so many others. Silence, synonymous with peace, actually tormented him. Words took shape only on the lips of others, and even when they held his hand, solitude still enveloped him, as if the world spoke a language he could never hear.

Jesus left the region near the city of Tyre, passed through Sidon and the region of Decapolis, and came to the Sea of Galilee. Some people brought a man who was deaf and could hardly speak and begged Jesus to lay His hand on him. Jesus took him aside from the crowd, put His fingers in the man's ears, and touched his tongue with saliva. Then He looked up to heaven, sighed deeply, and said to the man:
— "Ephphatha!" (This means: "Be opened!")
At that moment, the man's ears were opened, his tongue was loosened, and he began to speak without difficulty. Jesus commanded them not to tell anyone what had happened; however, the more He ordered them, the more they spread the word about what had occurred. And all the people who heard it were greatly amazed and said:
— Everything He does, He does well; He even makes the deaf hear and the mute speak! Mark 7:31-35

He could see the words being formed on the lips of others and could even feel the vibration of the sounds when touched by their hands, but he couldn't hear any sound. This is the story of the man who was led from one place to another by his friends.

That man couldn't hear, but he perceived everything by sight. When Jesus moved him, he became curious to know what would happen. By touching his ears and tongue, Jesus communicated with him through signs, as if to say, "I am touching your ears because I will heal you and wetting your tongue because you will speak." However, the miracle didn't happen until Jesus declared the blessing over his life, saying, "Ephphatha!" When He touched him, the Lord created a deep connection with him, something that few healed by Jesus experienced.

I observe a similarity between this miracle and the text in Genesis 2:7, when God formed man from the dust of the earth. He could have created Adam simply by speaking, but He chose to shape him personally. Similarly, Jesus could have healed that man with just a word, but He chose to touch him, showing that he needed something more.

The first person to speak to that man was the Lord; the first voice, the first dialogue. Jesus no longer needed to use signs for him to understand. What a privilege that man received after so much time living in silence! After being healed, if they asked him what he heard for the first time, he could say, "I heard the sweet voice of a good man, the Son of God, who had compassion on me and brought me from solitude into full life." In the same way, He acts with us: when we hear His voice and understand the way of salvation, He transports us from solitude to His kingdom of love. Jesus could have performed that miracle where the man was, but He chose to bring him out of the crowd, indicating that something special was about to happen. When Jesus took him out of the crowd, he had the opportunity to be face to face with the Master. Now, it was just Jesus, him, and his problems. When we are alone with Jesus, our problems must go away, our diseases meet the One who heals, and our fears face the Prince of Peace.

Jesus touched his ears, touched his tongue, and changed his heart. On some occasions, He looked to the heavens as if to indicate that something divine was about to happen: a miracle. His deep sigh, revealed by the Greek word (στενάζω - stenázō), expressed a groan before crying out the word "Ephphatha!" With an inexpressible groan, Jesus cried out to the Father, as the Holy Spirit groans for us with inexpressible groans. By sighing, He expressed all the compassion He felt for that suffering man.

What was blocked was opened, and the man's greatest problem received an order to disappear. Deafness and difficulty in speaking were great challenges in his life. By healing his speech, Jesus gave him the opportunity to testify about the Lord's grace and mercy.

Faith comes by hearing, and hearing by the word of God. However, that man didn't have the privilege of hearing the wonders of God. His faith could only come by seeing the miracles of Jesus. We don't know if he followed Jesus from other places or if, on that very day, he witnessed the miracles of Jesus.

Because of his inability, people would lead him by the hand. When Jesus took him out of the crowd, I believe He also led him by the hand. The help seemed the same, but while he was being guided by people, nothing changed. It was when Jesus guided him out of the crowd that his life changed. The help from people was limited and only fed his dependence. After the miracle, the one who needed help became independent, and the one who was trapped in solitude was now free. A new world was before him.

Have you ever noticed how a child listens to new sounds? I believe he was like a child, surprised by the sounds of nature and, especially, the sound of the voices of the people he loved. Knowing that someone loves you is already good, but this is even better. Jesus didn't just give him a new life; He also gave him a new voice. The people who knew him before, when asking what happened, could hear from him: "The 'Ephphatha' of Jesus happened in my life." All suffering was changed in just one encounter, one word, one gesture from the Lord Jesus.

The paths that were closed and the opportunities that were blocked in that man's life were opened by the Lord's mercy. In the same way, our blockages and challenges will open if Jesus is by our side.

What stood out to you the most?

_____

_____

_____

_____

_____

How can this reflection enhance your spiritual life?

_____

_____

_____

_____

_____

_____

What would you say to Jesus today?

_____

_____

_____

_____

_____

_____

"Then who in the world can be saved?" He replied,
"What is impossible for people is possible with God."
Luke 18:26b-27

THE SECOND MULTIPLICATION

For three days they followed hope, and it did not disappoint them. Together in hunger, they were many, but when the miracles happened, they no longer remembered their sorrows. How could they be sad in the face of so many miracles? A few loaves and some fish were enough to fill overflowing baskets.

Jesus left there and went to the Sea of Galilee. Then He went up a mountainside and sat down. Great crowds came to Him, bringing the lame, the crippled, the blind, the mute, and many others. They laid them at His feet, and He healed them all. The people were amazed when they saw the mute speaking, the crippled made well, the lame walking, and the blind seeing. And they praised the God of Israel.
Jesus called His disciples to Him and said:
— I have compassion for these people; they have already been with Me for three days and have nothing to eat. I do not want to send them away hungry, or they may collapse on the way.
The disciples answered:
— Where could we get enough bread in this remote place to feed such a crowd?
— How many loaves do you have? — Jesus asked.
— Seven loaves and a few small fish! — they replied.
Then Jesus told the crowd to sit down on the ground. He took the seven loaves and the fish, gave thanks, broke them, and gave them to the disciples, and they in turn distributed them to the people. They all ate and were satisfied. Afterward, the disciples picked up seven baskets full of broken pieces that were left over. The number of those who ate was four thousand men, besides women and children.
After Jesus had sent the crowd away, He got into the boat and went to the region of Magadan. Matthew 15:29-39

They all came

For three days they remained, eyes fixed on the Master, hands raised, frail bodies but awakened hearts. The sick found healing and the crowd, praise. Hunger grew, the desert weighed on their steps. Four thousand men, perhaps twice as many, women, children, hope in their eyes. They did not come out of tradition but from the need for healing and deliverance.
Jesus was near the Sea of Galilee, possibly in the Decapolis, a region inhabited by Gentiles. This indicates that His ministry was not limited to the Jews. The crowd included four thousand men, not counting women and children, possibly reaching around ten thousand people. Far from the Pharisees and distant from the synagogues, Jesus was able to help the people, healing and delivering them.

Jesus and the mountain

It is interesting to note that many important moments in the life of Jesus took place on mountains: the Sermon on the Mount, the two multiplications, the Transfiguration, the triumphal entry, the crucifixion and the ascension. On this occasion, Jesus also went up a mountain, and the crowds gathered, bringing the sick. The people were amazed by the greatness of the miracles and praised God.

The Master's feeling

Unlike the first multiplication, the crowds stayed with Jesus for three consecutive days to the point of having nothing left to eat. Then we see Jesus express what He felt—not that He did not show His feelings, but this time He says: "I have compassion for these people," once again teaching the disciples that those people, like any others, were worthy of love and compassion.
Jesus did not want them to return on the road without food, due to the risk of fainting from hunger along the way. The Lord's care was not only spiritual but also material. Many think that God cares

only about our spiritual life, but Jesus showed that this is not true. His compassion is complete, both spiritual and physical. When Jesus says, "I do not want to send them away hungry," it means the same.

What shall we do?

The disciples asked: "Where could we find enough food in this desert to feed all these people?" In the first multiplication, the disciples wanted to send the crowd away so they could buy food for themselves, but Jesus ordered them to feed the people. This time, they chose not to give an opinion and let Jesus decide what to do. It was not a lack of faith or forgetfulness of the first event—they simply decided to place the problem in Jesus' hands. It was not wrong for them to have doubts, as they were learning that Jesus always had a solution for their problems. When we do not know what to do or do not understand what is happening, we should do as the disciples did and ask Jesus what to do.

What do you have?

Jesus was aware of what He was doing but still gave people the opportunity to interact with Him before performing His miracles. Our participation is essential to receiving our miracles: our faith and patience determine when and how we will be blessed. God wants us to have a relationship with Him based on intimacy and full trust, for without faith it is impossible to please God. Seven loaves, a few fish and faith in the Lord's hands. He breaks the bread, shares the grace and the little becomes abundance. Empty hands now hold baskets, full of leftovers, full of life. The crowd departs, satisfied. The boat set sail for Magadan, and the miracles remained engraved in memory, in their eyes and in their hearts. They returned to their homes, but on the sand remained the footprints of a people who witnessed an extraordinary event.

119

What stood out to you the most?

_____

_____

_____

_____

_____

How can this reflection enhance your spiritual life?

_____

_____

_____

_____

What would you say to Jesus today?

_____

_____

_____

_____

_____

_____

"For you know the grace of our Lord Jesus Christ, that though He was rich, yet for your sake He became poor, so that through His poverty you might become rich."
2 Corinthians 8:9

THE BLIND MAN OF BETHSAIDA

The light did not shine for him. His eyes were sad, and he was always guided wherever he went. Then, the gentle touch of grace and the saliva met, and what did not exist began to slowly return. The world was revealed in vivid colors, and the man saw the Author of Life for the first time. Darkness gave way to the light of faith.

Then Jesus and the disciples came to the village of Bethsaida. Some people brought a blind man and begged Jesus to touch him. He took the blind man by the hand and led him out of the village. Then He spit, put saliva on the man's eyes, laid His hands on him and asked:
— Do you see anything?
The man looked up and said:
— I see people; they look like trees, but they are walking around. Jesus placed His hands on the man's eyes again. This time, the blind man looked intently and was healed; then he began to see everything clearly. Then Jesus sent the man home with the instruction:
— Do not go back into the village or tell anyone there! Mark 8:22-26

This miracle is brief but full of details and peculiarities. We notice that it differs from the others performed by Jesus. Here, He intervened in two stages, while in many cases He healed instantly with a word, a touch or a command. Although there are similarities with other healings, this episode stands out for its particularities, making it unique among the miracles of Jesus. Everything suggests that this man was not born blind, for as soon as he began to see, he already recognized what was around him. He may have lost his sight over time, as he recognized trees and shapes. This man walked three distinct paths in his journey, and each of them represented a stage in his life.

The journey of dependence

In other miracles of healing the blind, we see that they cried out: "Jesus, Son of David!" insisting until they were heard when the Lord passed by. However, this man was brought to Jesus by people who accompanied him. Thus, his first walk was made in the company of those who led him. During that journey, they probably said to him: "We'll take you to the village, Jesus is there and He can heal you." Until that moment, he was totally dependent on others to live and move. Being blind in that culture meant being seen as a beggar, someone cursed. The culture itself despised people with physical disabilities, but Jesus did not despise him. On the contrary, He desired a personal and unique encounter with him.

Toward the miracle

The second walk was when Jesus took his hand and led him out of the village. Surely, that was a unique moment in this miracle. Can you imagine going through hardships, trials, and Jesus comes, holds your hand and says: "Come with me, let's walk together"?

Jesus wanted to take him out of that environment, out of that village — perhaps it was a place of unbelief. Many times, we are stuck in environments that prevent us from seeing the miracle, and Jesus invites us to hold His hand so He can take us to a place of rest.

How wonderful it is to have someone who loves us and leads us to our miracle! The walk wasn't short, because Jesus instructed him not to return to the village, which indicates that the village was far enough that people could not see them. What did Jesus ask this man? Jesus liked to interact through questions and to dialogue with the sick. While they walked, He may have asked: "What happened to you?" or "What do you want me to do for you?" Even though He knows our struggles, He wants to hear us.

Following in joy

The third and final walk reported in the text was the return home. Jesus said: "Do not go back into the village or tell anyone there!" This indicates that the man didn't live there. That joy was for him and his family. That walk was the happiest of his life, for he now had his miracle in hand.

Something interesting about this miracle is that Jesus did not act the same way as in other cases. He touched the blind man's eyes twice to fully restore his vision. The first time, when the man began to see, his faith must have increased, because he realized that something was happening. On the second touch, Jesus completed the work. Sometimes we feel that something has begun to change, but it seems like the miracle stopped halfway. However, Jesus keeps working, and at the right time, He will finish His work.

This blind man wasn't healed instantly. He needed to interact with Jesus. Jesus asked: "What do you see?" In the same way, there are moments when we need to talk with God, express our faith and share our doubts. The miracle doesn't happen with the snap of a finger, but in the time appointed by Him. The most important thing is to know that Jesus is working, even if in an unexpected way.

Think about the blind man's walk. When his friends brought him to Jesus, he hadn't yet received the miracle. Nevertheless, when he began to walk with Jesus, everything changed. How many times do we seek God for an answer and see nothing happen? It may be that we're only going to the place where Jesus is, but not truly walking with Him. Transformation happens when we begin to walk with Christ.

If we could draw one lesson from this miracle, it would be this: God has different ways of working. Your miracle may be similar to someone else's — a healing, a deliverance, a financial provision — but that doesn't mean He will act the same way every time. God has infinite ways to accomplish the impossible in our lives.

What stood out to you the most?

_____

_____

_____

_____

_____

How can this reflection enhance your spiritual life?

_____

_____

_____

_____

_____

What would you say to Jesus today?

_____

_____

_____

_____

_____

_____

"And we know that all things work together for the good of those who love God, of those who are called according to His purpose."
Romans 8:28–29

THE TRANSFIGURATION

To a few He revealed Himself fully, even though they were not yet matured. Three saw, and three-thirds only heard. An unusual cloud, from which no rain came, but the voice of the Almighty. To see, they had to walk, and to understand, believe. The climb was difficult, the night dark and their eyelids weary, but the descent was joyful and full of hope. The lives of these men could be divided into: before the vision and after it. "Tell no one anything," He said.

Six days later, Jesus went up a high mountain, taking only Peter and the brothers James and John with Him. There, they saw the appearance of Jesus change: His face shone like the sun, and His clothes became as white as the light. And the three disciples saw Moses and Elijah talking with Jesus. Then Peter said to Jesus,
— Lord, how good it is for us to be here! If You wish, I will put up three shelters: one for You, one for Moses, and one for Elijah.
While Peter was still speaking, a bright cloud covered them, and a voice came from the cloud, saying,
— This is My beloved Son, in whom I am well pleased. Listen to Him!
When the disciples heard the voice, they were so frightened that they fell on their faces to the ground. Jesus came, touched them, and said,
— Get up, and do not be afraid!
When they looked up, they saw no one except Jesus. As they were coming down the mountain, Jesus instructed them,
— Do not tell anyone what you have seen until the Son of Man has been raised from the dead. Matthew 17:1-9

The Transfiguration is one of the most glorious moments in the New Testament, where Jesus reveals His divine glory before the disciples, and the Father speaks about the Son through a cloud of glory, just like at the baptism of Jesus. The voice of the Almighty was heard as a testimony of His ministry.

Several characters took part in this event: Peter, James, John, and the prophets Elijah and Moses. Peter, astonished, wanted to make three shelters for Jesus, Elijah, and Moses, placing them on the same level. He still did not understand the true position of Jesus as Lord. The presence of Moses and Elijah symbolized the Law and the Prophets, for Jesus came to fulfill the Law and accomplish the prophecies about the Messiah.

It was not by chance that God chose Moses and Elijah to be there. These prophets had intimacy with God and spoke directly to Him. Their ministries had similarities: both had authority over nature. Moses parted the Red Sea; Elijah divided the waters of the Jordan River with his cloak. However, Jesus, greater than them, did not need to part the waters, for He walked on them.

Moreover, Moses, Elijah, and Jesus were the only ones in the Bible who fasted for forty days. However, Jesus was the only one who was tempted by Satan at the end of that period. The Transfiguration was the moment when heaven descended and met the Earth, the moment when God reaffirmed: "This is My beloved Son!" Peter was so impacted that he forgot everything around him. He didn't remember relatives or the other disciples. He wanted to stay there because that atmosphere carried the essence of heaven.

In the three synoptic Gospels, we see how each one described the light radiating from Jesus. Matthew says His face shone like the sun, and His clothes became as white as the light. Luke states that His appearance was transformed, and His clothes shone like lightning. Mark emphasizes that His clothes became whiter than any launderer on Earth could bleach them. Each one tried to describe something indescribable, for only those who saw could understand the manifested glory.

Another important detail is God's command: "Listen to Him." God was telling us to pay attention to the message of Jesus. Today, many talk about Moses, Elijah, and the prophets, but forget to listen to what Jesus taught. God's command is clear: listen to

Jesus! And more than listening, we must transmit this message to others.

The Transfiguration connects to three other great supernatural testimonies about Jesus. During His birth, the angel announced: 'I bring you good news that will cause great joy: today in the town of David a Savior has been born to you; He is the Messiah, the Lord' (Luke 2:11). When He was baptized, God declared: 'This is My beloved Son, in whom I am well pleased' (Matthew 3:17). During the Transfiguration, God repeated this affirmation, adding: 'Listen to Him.'"

Luke 9:31 mentions that Moses and Elijah spoke about Jesus' "departure." In the original Greek, this word is "exodus." Just as Moses led the people in the exodus toward the Promised Land, Jesus would open the way for the salvation of humanity. His sacrifice represented a new spiritual exodus, leading us back to God.

Matthew 17:2 says that Jesus was transfigured. In the original, the word used is "metamorphosis." He underwent a glorious transformation, anticipating what will happen to all those who are in Christ, going through a spiritual transformation.

Another notable similarity: Elijah was taken to heaven before Elisha, and Jesus also ascended before His disciples. These events show that the Transfiguration was not a random occurrence, but an event full of divine symbolism.

This event must be studied carefully, for it reveals many spiritual truths. Only three disciples participated in this moment: Peter, James, and John. They were the closest to Jesus, always by His side. This teaches us that those who walk closer to Jesus experience deeper revelations.

In Matthew 17:6, we see that the disciples were terrified when they heard the voice of God and fell with their faces to the ground. Then Jesus came, touched them, and said: "Get up, do not be afraid." This shows us that when we are with Jesus, there is no reason to fear, for His hand will lift us up.

Many times, we forget that we are with Jesus and let fear dominate us. He helps us and encourages us to rise. There are moments when we need to get up from our prostration and understand that Jesus is by our side and cry out: "Lord, lift me up!"

God's presence will always be awe-inspiring to human beings, for no one can see God face to face. The disciples' fear is justified for this reason, but it was a result of human insecurity. When Jesus arrived, He dispelled all fear. The love of God casts out all fear. When we trust in that love, we understand that He cares for us and can do infinitely more than we ask or imagine.

The great lesson we take from this is: if we are with Jesus and His Word is in us, there will always be miracles in our lives. In the presence of Jesus, there is healing, restoration, restitution, comfort, and deliverance from fear.

Those disciples saw the light of Jesus, not only with their physical eyes but with their spiritual eyes, for the light of salvation is the most important. They had a glimpse of a glorified body. The Apostle Paul, in his letter to the Philippians, writes: "But our citizenship is in heaven, and we eagerly await a Savior from there, the Lord Jesus Christ, who, by the power that enables Him to bring everything under His control, will transform our lowly bodies so that they will be like His glorious body" (Philippians 3:20-21).

Finally, Jesus declares in John 12:46: "I am the light of the world. Whoever follows Me will never walk in darkness, but will have the light of life."

What stood out to you the most?

_____

_____

_____

_____

_____

How can this reflection enhance your spiritual life?

_____

_____

_____

_____

_____

What would you say to Jesus today?

_____

_____

_____

_____

_____

"Casting all your anxiety on Him, because He cares for you. Be sober-minded! Watchful! For your adversary the devil walks around like a roaring lion, seeking whom he may devour. Resist him, standing firm in the faith, knowing that the same sufferings are being experienced by your brothers throughout the world."
1 Peter 5:7–9

THE DEMON-POSSESSED BOY

In the anguishing silence of a desperate father, a child struggles against invisible forces that lead her to the fire and to the water, as if her destiny were determined by destruction. The life of an innocent being is threatened by an evil that no one knows how to control. As she approaches Jesus, hope is reborn. With a gesture of love, compassion, and authority, He organizes the chaos, bringing healing, peace, and liberation.

When they arrived [Jesus, Peter, James, and John, descending from the Mount of Transfiguration] near the other disciples, they saw a large crowd around them and some teachers of the law arguing with them. When the people saw Jesus, they were all amazed and ran to greet Him. Jesus asked the disciples:
— What are you arguing with them about?
A man in the crowd answered:
— Teacher, I brought my son to You because he is possessed by an evil spirit and cannot speak. Whenever the spirit attacks my son, it throws him to the ground, and he starts foaming at the mouth and grinding his teeth; and he is getting weaker and weaker. I asked Your disciples to drive out the spirit, but they couldn't.
Jesus said:
— O unbelieving generation! How long shall I stay with you? How long shall I put up with you? Bring the boy to Me.
When they brought him, the spirit saw Jesus and immediately threw the boy into a convulsion. He fell to the ground and rolled around, foaming at the mouth. Jesus asked the boy's father:
— How long has he been like this?
The father answered:
— From childhood. Many times it has thrown him into the fire or water to kill him. But if You can do anything, take pity on us and help us.

Jesus said:

— If you can? Everything is possible for one who believes.

Immediately the boy's father exclaimed:

— I do believe; help me overcome my unbelief!

When Jesus saw that a crowd was running to the scene, He rebuked the impure spirit.

— You deaf and mute spirit, He said, I command you, come out of him and never enter him again.

The spirit shrieked, convulsed the boy violently and came out. The boy looked so much like a corpse that many said, "He's dead." But Jesus took him by the hand and lifted him to his feet, and he stood up.

After Jesus had gone indoors, His disciples asked Him privately,

— Why couldn't we drive it out?

He replied,

— Because you have so little faith. Truly I tell you, if you have faith as small as a mustard seed, you can say to this mountain, "Move from here to there," and it will move. Nothing will be impossible for you.

Mark 9:14-29, Matthew 17:19-21

This miracle is clearly divided into two parts. The first is a theological discussion between the scribes and the disciples. The second part is the miracle, where Jesus frees the boy from the evil spirit that tormented him, showing His power of healing and deliverance.

This event takes place right after the Transfiguration, when Jesus took Peter, James, and John to the mountain, and there His glory was revealed. Upon descending from the mountain, Jesus finds the other disciples arguing with the scribes. When He asks what they were discussing, the boy's father explains that the disciples were unable to drive out the spirit, which caused Jesus' indignation. He had already given authority to the disciples to cast out demons, as had happened before.

However, they were unable to cast out this spirit, and Jesus makes it clear that the problem was a lack of faith. "If you can believe, all things are possible."

We understand that the lack of faith was crucial in their inability to perform the miracle. Jesus, with indignation, says, "O unbelieving generation, how long shall I be with you?" He was tired of dealing with the lack of faith, especially after three years of ministry. The unbelief of the disciples and the other religious leaders caused sorrow in His heart.

When Jesus encounters the boy, the spirit in him immediately manifests, as if it knew it could not resist the presence of Jesus. This teaches us that when we are in Christ, darkness cannot remain. The light of Christ dispels all darkness. Jesus then casts out the spirit, saying, "Come out of him and never enter him again." This is the authority that Christ has also given us. When dealing with the spiritual world, we must always say, "…and never come back."

The culminating moment occurs when Jesus takes the boy's hand and lifts him up. This teaches us that even in our lowest moments, when we are fallen, defeated, or downcast, if we take the hand of Jesus, He will lift us up and make us stand. No matter how difficult the circumstances, if we have faith in Jesus, He will never leave us helpless. Our faith is what makes the impossible possible.

If you find yourself in an impossible situation, know that faith in Christ can transform any situation. What we often lack is the belief. Jesus challenges us by saying, "If you can believe." The boy's father, despite his doubt, cried out, "I believe; help my unbelief." Sometimes, our faith is small, but it is in the sincere cry that God works.

Faith comes by hearing the Word of God. If you want to increase your faith, begin to meditate on God's promises. Open the Bible and seek the promises He has for your life. Do not be discouraged by difficulties, for God is faithful to fulfill His promises and raise us from the ground.

What stood out to you the most?

_____

_____

_____

_____

_____

How can this reflection enhance your spiritual life?

_____

_____

_____

_____

_____

What would you say to Jesus today?

_____

_____

_____

_____

_____

_____

*"Blessed be the God and Father of our Lord Jesus
Christ, the Father of mercies and God of all comfort, who
comforts us in all our tribulations, so that we may be able to
comfort those who are in any trouble, with the comfort with
which we ourselves are comforted by God."*
2 Corinthians 1:3–4

PETER AND THE COIN

In the calm lake, he casts his hook, unaware of what he might find. The still waters would reveal the miracle that would surface. The fish and the coin appear as an answer to a need, a divine provision. There were no visible signs, but faith was revealed in the simple act of obedience. That fish, carrying the solution within itself, was more than a surprise; it was a reminder that, in moments of uncertainty, God finds unexpected ways to care for us. The impossible becomes possible, and trust in His power leads us to the miracle.

When Jesus and the disciples arrived in the city of Capernaum, the collectors of the Temple tax came to ask Peter:
— Doesn't your Master pay the Temple tax?
— Yes, He does! — Peter replied.
Then Peter went into the house, but before he said anything, Jesus said:
— Simon, what do you think? Who pays duties and taxes to the kings of this world? The citizens of the country or the foreigners?
— The foreigners! — Peter answered.
— That's right! — said Jesus. — That means the citizens don't have to pay. But we don't want to offend these people. So go to the lake, cast a hook, and pull up the first fish you catch. In its mouth you will find a coin. Take it and pay the tax for Me and for you.
Matthew 17:24-27

This episode about taxes teaches us that sometimes it's better to take a longer route to avoid conflict or offense. Jesus, as a Jew, was not obligated to pay that tax because it was collected only from foreigners. However, by analyzing everything involved, Jesus chose to pay it, to honor Peter's promise to the collectors and put an end to the issue. The Lord's wisdom in resolving problems with simplicity and humility serves as an example for us. Sometimes, actions that cost us just a few extra minutes can save us from unnecessary problems and fruitless arguments. Our time and our personal relationships are important factors in our lives because they help us achieve our goals. What we need least are enemies and discussions that lead nowhere.

Jesus understood that He shouldn't have to pay this tax, and the text doesn't clearly name the tax, but as the Son of God, He was heir to all things. It's like the heir of a company going with a friend to one of his stores. Upon arriving, he picks something for himself and his friend. As they leave, someone, not knowing he's the heir, asks, "Aren't you going to pay for what you took?" The friend looks at the owner's son, and he says, "Go and pay, because these people don't know us." Those men didn't understand Jesus' greatness, which is why Jesus said, "Go and pay for Me and for you." Jesus was, in fact, acting exactly as He taught in the Sermon on the Mount when He said, "if anyone wants to sue you and take your tunic, hand over your cloak as well." Matthew 5:40

This miracle is different from all others because it was the only miracle Jesus performed together with a disciple. It's interesting to note how Peter is part of so many unique situations. He was the only disciple who walked on water, the only one to be harshly rebuked by Jesus, and once again, Peter was with Jesus in a singular moment. Unlike the others, this miracle also helped Jesus.

Peter was only able to pay the taxes because he was with Jesus. There are situations we will only overcome if we are walking with Jesus. How wonderful it is to walk with Jesus, because there is no lack He cannot supply. If we are walking with Him, obeying and believing in His word, we will receive the miracle, just as Peter did.

I see three characteristics in the actions of the apostle Peter. First, he obeyed. Second, he believed the word given to him. Finally, he acted. If Peter had stayed still, not going to the lake or casting the hook into the water, he would not have seen the miracle happen. Imagine if someone approached and asked, "Peter, are you fishing again? What kind of fish do you expect to catch?"

Surely, Peter wouldn't say something like, "I'm fishing here because my Lord said that if I cast the hook, a fish will come up with money in its mouth." He simply believed, obeyed, and acted, trusting that the miracle would happen.

This miracle was a partnership: Jesus received His part, and Peter received his. Peter received first because he was walking with Jesus. He was in the right place, at the right time, and with the right company. He obeyed, believed, and acted. He was walking with Jesus, following the instruction, and believing in the word given to him. When he reaped the fruit of his faith, he didn't just help himself, but also helped Jesus.

There is a partnership we form with God regarding His work and His church. Jesus speaks the word: "Go into all the world and preach the gospel to every creature." When you obey, you win souls for God and for the church. This is a partnership in which both you and the Kingdom gain. However, we need to walk with Jesus for this partnership to succeed. We must act according to the spoken word, the established promises, and the teachings of Jesus.

If I were to draw out one key lesson—though I see many—I would say the key teaching from this miracle is this: Peter received his miracle because he was walking side by side with Jesus, obeying the instruction, and believing the spoken word. What is the word that Jesus has spoken over your life? What has Jesus asked of us? What has He promised? Just believe in the word spoken by the Master, because God's word never returns empty.

There are many promises for us, left by God in His word. There are many promises from Jesus in the New Testament, reserved for us—the church of the final hour. Just trust, because what is your need? Peter's need was to pay the taxes. What is your need? We all have needs: some small, some enormous, and some that seem impossible to meet. However, follow the example of the disciple Peter, who, walking with Jesus, obeyed His word. He believed in the instruction and acted, trusting that by doing what

Jesus said, he would receive what was promised. The word of God does not return empty; the word of God is fulfilled. Therefore, we must believe in Jesus' instructions.

How many times do we face the unexpected? Peter would never have imagined that his provision would be inside the mouth of a fish. Just as God worked a miracle through Jesus' word—an unusual, unexpected, never-before-seen miracle—He can do the same in our lives. An unexpected miracle, one that has never happened to anyone else, but will happen to you. Do you know why? Because if you walk with Jesus, believe in His word, and follow His instructions, the word of Jesus will be fulfilled. The word of the miracle will come to pass.

Peter believed and acted, and everything became possible. He went believing, cast the hook believing, and pulled the fish up believing. When he opened the fish's mouth, he saw his miracle.

What stood out to you the most?

_____

_____

_____

_____

_____

How can this reflection enhance your spiritual life?

_____

_____

_____

_____

_____

_____

What would you say to Jesus today?

_____

_____

_____

_____

_____

_____

"He has delivered us from the power of darkness and conveyed us into the kingdom of the Son of His love, in whom we have redemption through His blood, the forgiveness of sins."
Colossians 1:13-14

THE MAN BORN BLIND

As He walked, He saw a forgotten man, blind from birth. He asked for nothing, did not cry out, sought nothing, yet he was found. With mud and steps of obedience, he walked toward his destiny. Darkness gave way to light, and shame to recognition. Once forgotten, now he was admired by all. No one cared about him—until he was touched. Now, he had a story to tell. What was once rejected became a vision of divine power. That man's darkness was filled with a light no one could deny. He obeyed, saw, and only then believed. A touch not only opened his eyes but also revealed a new life. Because where everyone saw only abandonment, Jesus declared hope and purpose.

The Word commands: "Go and wash." Hesitant steps follow, but faith walks firmly. Water flows, and the miracle unfolds—light bursts in, colors arise, faces take shape. What once was shadow becomes clarity. The forgotten is seen, the invisible remembered, and the poor blind man becomes a witness of what the touch of the Sent One can do.

Jesus was walking along when He saw a man who had been blind since birth. His disciples asked:

— Teacher, why was this man born blind? Was it because of his sins or because of his parents' sins?

Jesus answered:

— He is blind, yes, but not because of his sins nor his parents' sins. He is blind so that the power of God may be shown in him. We must work while it is day to do the works of the One who sent Me. Night is coming, when no one can work. While I am in the world, I am the light of the world.

After saying this, Jesus spat on the ground, made some mud with the saliva, put the mud on the blind man's eyes and said:

— Go wash your face in the Pool of Siloam. (This name means "The One Who Was Sent.")

The blind man went, washed his face and came back seeing.

His neighbors and those who were used to seeing him begging asked:

— Isn't this the man who used to sit and beg?

— Yes! — some said.

— No, it isn't. But he looks like him! — others affirmed. But he said:

— It's me.

— How is it that you can see now? — they asked.

He answered:

— The man called Jesus made some mud, put it on my eyes and said: "Go to the Pool of Siloam and wash your face." So I went, washed my face and could see.

— Where is that man? — they asked.

— I don't know! — he replied.

Then they took the man who had been blind to the Pharisees.

The day Jesus had made the mud and healed the man from blindness was a Sabbath.

So the Pharisees also asked how he had been healed.

— He put mud on my eyes, I washed my face and now I can see — the man answered.

Some of the Pharisees said:

— The man who did this is not from God because He doesn't respect the Sabbath law.

And others asked:

— How can a sinner do such great miracles?

So there was division among them.

Then the Pharisees asked the man again:

— You say He healed you from blindness. What do you say about Him?

— He is a prophet! — the man replied.

The Jewish leaders didn't believe he had been blind and that he could now see. So they called his parents and asked:

— Is this your son? Do you say he was born blind? Then how is he seeing now?

The parents replied:

— We know he is our son and that he was born blind.

But we don't know how he can see now and we also don't know who healed him. He is of age; ask him and he can explain himself.

The parents said this because they were afraid, as the Jewish leaders had agreed to expel from the synagogue anyone who declared that Jesus was the Messiah.

That's why the parents said: "He is of age; ask him."

So the Jewish leaders called the man who had been blind a second time and said:

— Swear by God that you will tell the truth. We know that this man is a sinner. He replied:

— Whether He is a sinner, I don't know. One thing I do know: I was blind and now I can see!

— What did He do to you? How did He heal your blindness? — they asked again. The man replied:

— I've already told you and you didn't believe. Why do you want to hear it again? Could it be that you also want to be His followers?

Then they insulted him and said:

— You're His follower! We are followers of Moses. We know God spoke to Moses, but as for this man, we don't even know where He comes from. He replied:

— What a strange thing! You don't know where He comes from, but He healed me. We know that God doesn't listen to sinners, but He listens to those who fear Him and do His will. Since the world began, no one has ever heard of someone healing a man born blind. If this man were not sent by God, He could do nothing.

They replied:

— You were born full of sin, and you want to teach us? And they expelled him from the synagogue.

Jesus heard that they had expelled the man from the synagogue. He went looking for him and when He found him, He asked:

— Do you believe in the Son of Man?

He answered:
— Lord, who is the Son of Man so I can believe in Him?
Jesus said:
— You have seen Him! He is the one speaking to you!
— I believe, Lord! — the man said. And he knelt before Him.
Then Jesus said:
*— I came into this world to judge people, so that the blind may
see and those who see may become blind.*
Some Pharisees who were with Him heard this and asked:
— Does this mean that we are blind too?
*— If you were blind, you wouldn't be guilty! — Jesus replied. —
But since you say that you can see, your guilt remains.*
John 9:1–41

This miracle is one of the richest, most complete, and longest in Jesus' ministry. There are forty-one verses detailing this episode that transformed the life of this man. Many lessons can be drawn from this account! Three parts are clearly divided: the miracle, the religious discussion between the Pharisees, and the salvation of the man who was blind. The Pharisees hated Jesus because He healed on the Sabbath and because the people followed Him and called Him a prophet — which He truly was. Out of pride, they rejected Jesus.

This man did nothing to receive his miracle. He didn't seek Jesus, didn't speak to Jesus, and didn't beg for healing, but God had an appointment with him. When Jesus said that this situation was for God's power to be manifested in him, that's exactly what happened. He was poor, blind, despised, and on top of all that, a beggar. He was so ignored that, after his healing, people didn't even recognize him. John, in fact, didn't record his name, demonstrating how unknown he was to society. However, Jesus saw him, and he wasn't forgotten by the Lord.

The text suggests that he didn't have perfect eyes, as the disciples immediately identified that he was blind from birth; his eye sockets were probably defective. When Jesus spat on the ground, made mud, and applied it to his eyes, He may have filled those empty sockets. Then, He sent him to the Pool of Siloam, which means "Sent." Thus, Jesus, the Sent One of God, sent the blind man to the pool called "Sent," making that man also a sent one.

This man was obedient: he didn't question, doubt, or complain. He simply went and obeyed. When asked about his healing, he replied: "I only know that I was blind, and now I see." He wasn't concerned with understanding how the miracle happened; he just testified that he was healed.

By noticing that he didn't ask to be healed, we're simply observing the text itself; we don't know if he had cried out to God for healing throughout his life, but he was just in the right place. We understand that his blindness was so severe that the text says that a healing like that had never happened before. Throughout his life, he may have heard that his blindness was so severe that it would be impossible to heal.

We will never know for sure beyond what the Bible tells us, but one thing is certain: God had mercy on that man, and just as He had mercy on him, He has mercy on us as long as we are in the right place.

The only thing Jesus received from him was his firm and faithful testimony. He didn't fear the religious leaders and, unlike his parents, he confronted them with irrefutable facts, such as: "I was blind, and now I see" and "God doesn't listen to sinners, but He listens to those who fear Him and do His will." Just two of his arguments were enough to destroy the pride and false accusations of the Pharisees. The Lord Jesus sees those who are forgotten and abandoned, and it doesn't matter how long we have been waiting for a miracle. If you suffer like this, know that Jesus sees you and can change your story, just as He changed that man's story on a day when he perhaps least expected it.

What stood out to you the most?

_____

_____

_____

_____

_____

How can this reflection enhance your spiritual life?

_____

_____

_____

_____

What would you say to Jesus today?

_____

_____

_____

_____

"For He Himself has said: I will never leave you nor forsake you. So we may boldly say: The Lord is my helper; I will not fear. What can man do to me? Remember those who rule over you, who have spoken the word of God to you, whose faith follow, considering the outcome of their conduct. Jesus Christ is the same yesterday, today, and forever."
Hebrews 13:5-8

THE TEN LEPERS

The pain united the forgotten, and suffering transformed ten paths into one. Why walk many roads if the anguish is the same? Who would understand our pain, if not ourselves? Who would know what it is to be despised, cast out, and hated even by our own? Friends abandoned us, family let us down, but hope never left us alone. When we heard about Him, our voice was transformed. We no longer shouted "Unclean! Unclean!", but cried out, with hearts aflame: "Have mercy on us!"

Jesus was traveling to Jerusalem and passed between the regions of Samaria and Galilee. As He was entering a village, ten lepers met Him. They stopped at a distance and called out:
— Jesus, Master, have mercy on us!
Jesus saw them and said:
— Go and have the priests examine you.
As they went on their way, they were healed. And when one of them, a Samaritan, saw that he was healed, he returned, praising God in a loud voice. He knelt at Jesus' feet and thanked Him. Jesus said:
— Were not all ten healed? Where are the other nine? Why is it only this foreigner who returned to give praise to God?
And Jesus said to him:
— Get up and go. Your faith has healed you. Luke 17:11-19

To understand a bit about this illness, in Leviticus 13:44, we find the Mosaic law's instructions regarding leprosy. These recommendations aimed to avoid contamination among the people, so those affected by this disease were separated from the community and were forced to stay outside the village. Whenever an unsuspecting person approached, the leper had to warn them by shouting: "Unclean! Unclean!". They had four main guidelines: to stay away from the people, family, and the city, living in isolation; to wear torn clothes; to not comb their hair to cover the disease, letting it grow; and, when someone approached, to shout "Unclean!".

At that time, leprosy had no cure, and these people were rejected by the community, seen as sinners, cursed, and abandoned by all. They could not receive care from their families and lost everything. The condition of the leper was even worse than that of a beggar, because, despite suffering prejudice and rejection, a beggar could still live in society and near their family. Leprosy imposed perhaps the worst condition among all diseases.

If we compare the first leprosy healing in Mark 1:40, we see that Jesus acted differently. In the first case, Jesus touched and healed immediately. In the second, Jesus spoke a prophetic word: "Go and show yourselves to the priest." The priests were responsible for sanitary inspections and followed a specific process. When someone showed symptoms of leprosy, the priest would examine and, if necessary, isolate the person until confirming whether they were healed or not. When Jesus ordered the lepers to present themselves to the priest, they believed they would be healed, certain that when they reached the priest, they would say: "Jesus healed us and sent us here to be examined."

Curiously, they were not healed immediately, but along the way. Jesus then asked: "Were not ten healed? Where are the other nine?" Although it's easy to criticize the nine who didn't return, the truth is that, even though they did not express gratitude, they obeyed the Lord. However, they lost the opportunity to thank. Nevertheless, they were healed because they believed and obeyed Jesus' word. And often, this is how we receive our miracles: by obeying God's word, believing in His promises, and living in obedience and faith.

When that man returned to thank, he received a second blessing. Jesus said to him: "Get up and go, your faith has healed you." Imagine the privilege of receiving from the Savior Himself the declaration that he was saved! The other nine received only physical healing, but this man received both healing and salvation. He not only obeyed but returned to thank and recognize Jesus as

Lord. This act of gratitude resulted in something very special: he was declared saved by Jesus Himself. The word used for "saved" in the original Greek text is "sōzō," meaning complete, healed, delivered, and restored.

This was the greatest blessing: when he returned to thank, he received from Jesus Himself the declaration that he was saved. The other nine left healed, but only that man — a Samaritan, someone seen as a second-class Jew, despised and discriminated against — was saved. This teaches us that it doesn't matter our condition, nationality, or origin. What matters is the faith and obedience that place us in the right position to receive the miracle.

Certainly, after this encounter with Jesus, that man went to reunite with his friends and family. Perhaps someone asked: "Where did you go?" And he must have replied: "I went to thank my healing, and the Lord said I was saved."

Life gives us the opportunity to thank God for all the blessings we have. We receive deliverance, prosperity, health, and many other miracles, and sometimes we forget to return to the Savior to thank and worship Him. That Samaritan knelt at Jesus' feet, giving thanks. If there is one lesson from this miracle, it is this: it is on the path of obedience that we receive our miracles. It wasn't at the beginning or at the end, but during the journey that those men were healed. They didn't know when they would be healed, but they were going in the right direction and acting in faith.

On that day, the village was filled with ten stories of joy. By humanizing these lepers, we can imagine some of these stories, such as: the story of a wife hanging clothes on the line and her husband appearing at the gate of the house, clean and healed; a mother feeding her baby while hearing, after a long time, the voice of her husband echoing through the house; the daughter playing in her room when the door slowly opens, and her father appears smiling; a woman looking from a distance, beginning to see someone walking as if it were her son: "This couldn't be my son, he's a leper and lives outside the village... But the walk is the same, and the appearance is the same!"; a father sitting at the table, and when he looks, he sees his beloved son entering the house after such a long time; the boy kicking his ball to see it stop at his father's feet; the woman who was a fiancée and couldn't marry, hearing the news that all the lepers of the village were healed, including her fiancé.

Can you imagine the greatness of this miracle? Ten families received their loved ones back. The mercy of Jesus saw these stories, and even without gratitude, His love did not make distinctions between them. Both the grateful and the forgotten received a great blessing. However, the one who returned to thank had a unique experience with the Savior. That man was the only one to understand the greatness of the Master. Not only the greatness but also the worthiness of gratitude. Among all the people he could run to embrace, he chose to invest those precious moments of health to give thanks to the Lord.

The other nine will always be remembered for their ingratitude, but the one who thanked will be recognized as the grateful man, no longer marked by the condition of curse and abandonment but exalted for his act of thanksgiving.

On that unusual night, ten families shared a meal full of stories, and however sad some of them were, they all ended with the restoration of their lives.

What stood out to you the most?

_____

_____

_____

_____

_____

How can this reflection enhance your spiritual life?

_____

_____

_____

_____

What would you say to Jesus today?

_____

_____

_____

_____

"Christ has redeemed us from the curse of the law, having become a curse for us (for it is written: Cursed is everyone who hangs on a tree), that the blessing of Abraham might come upon the Gentiles in Christ Jesus, that we might receive the promise of the Spirit through faith."
Galatians 3:13-14

THE DROPSICAL MAN

Among the teachers of the law was he; among the leaders of religion stood the one who, in everyone's eyes, was pitiful. His problem was visible and his affliction could not be hidden, but his pain he carried alone. Wherever he walked, he would be noticed not for his qualities, but for his disgrace. His body was different, even though his soul was the soul of a person. They debated whether his fate should change at that moment or wait for another day. Those who do not suffer can wait, but those who are in pain are in a hurry. To do good, the prophet hurried, and the one who could not answer had to silence his hypocrisy.

One Sabbath, Jesus went to eat at the house of a Pharisee leader, and the people there were watching Him closely. A man with swollen arms and legs came near Him. And Jesus asked the teachers of the Law and the Pharisees:
— Does our Law allow healing on the Sabbath or not?
But they said nothing. Then Jesus took hold of the man, healed him, and sent him away. Then He said:
— If a son or an ox of one of you falls into a pit, won't you pull him out immediately, even if it happens on a Sabbath?
And they could not answer. Luke 14:1-6

Dropsy is a disease that causes swelling due to fluid retention, making parts of the body appear swollen. In another version, we see the word "swollen," but we know the correct name of the disease is dropsy, and this condition caused the man to be separated and rejected by the people. This is because the Jews did not accept diseases or infirmities, since they believed in the covenant they had with God, described in Deuteronomy 28:2, where it is written: "All these blessings shall come upon you and overtake you, if you obey the voice of the Lord." There several blessings are listed, but in Deuteronomy 28:15, many curses are described.

The Jew believed that the curse was a consequence of the person's or the parents' sin. So when a Jew encountered someone who was sick, especially in the case of this man, he would immediately think: "He sinned, he is in sin, he is cursed" and would despise that person.

This is evident, for in a previous miracle, the disciples asked Jesus whether the blind man had sinned or his parents. Jesus answered: "Neither he nor his parents." Just like that blind man was rejected, this one was also rejected. Even today, we often try to find a reason in a person's life when something terrible happens to them. Sometimes there is an evident reason that results from a choice, but many times it is simply the affliction Jesus mentioned: "In this world you will have affliction, but take heart." We will all go through afflictions in one way or another. However, there is Jesus' promise: "Take heart," because He is with us.

That man was there, rejected and despised, yet the text says he was near Jesus. Despite the prejudice, he kept approaching and, little by little, got so close that Jesus touched him. At no time did Jesus despise that man; on the contrary, He chose to set him free. While men look at appearances, the Lord looked at him with compassion. Jesus didn't waste time because He wanted to interact with him, to bring him into a healthy and full life. He also wanted to deal with the Pharisees' hypocrisy. This issue of healing on the Sabbath appears seven times in Jesus' miracles, and on two occasions He asked, "Is it lawful to do good on the Sabbath?" The Pharisees were very rigid with the law, but at the same time, they were hypocrites because they did not truly follow it. Jesus pointed out that if a son or an ox of theirs fell into a pit on the Sabbath, they would pull it out. This revealed that the issue was not strictness with the law, but hypocrisy.

In another passage, Jesus said: "The Sabbath was made for man, not man for the Sabbath." The Sabbath was instituted to serve man as rest, not to make man its slave. Jesus affirmed: "I am Lord of the Sabbath." He cited the example of when David and his men ate the consecrated bread, which was not lawful to eat, in

Matthew 12:3. He taught that the priority was the human being, something the Pharisees, due to their hardened hearts, could not understand. That man knew and believed that Jesus could heal him. He stepped forward and put himself within Jesus' reach, willing to be healed. If he had stayed hidden, ashamed, or afraid of others' opinions, he might not have been healed. He could have been in the same house, but hidden in the back. However, the text says he was near.

Something interesting is that after Jesus healed him, He immediately sent him away. He shouldn't remain among those who didn't even want him to be healed. Jesus sent him to be with his family, with those who loved him. Sometimes, our enemies are closer than we imagine. They are the ones who don't believe in our miracle or who don't encourage us. In the case of the Pharisees, they didn't want that man to be healed. But he was near Jesus and, because of that, received his blessing.

Maybe you're asking: "How did they know that man was healed?" Because he was instantly unswollen. It was a visible miracle. The text says the Pharisees and the teachers of the law remained silent. When God performs your miracle, those who don't believe in Him will have no words.

That's what we must do: make ourselves available to the Lord, stay close to His Word and His will, because in doing so our chances multiply. It is impossible to be in the Lord's presence and leave the same. He will always do something on our behalf. All those who came into His presence with faith were healed.

As we meditate on the Lord's wonders, our faith is strengthened, for He is powerful and unchanging. The same Jesus who healed the man with dropsy is at work today and can move in your life. You just need to believe that He is powerful, righteous, and faithful, and that His goodness endures forever.

What stood out to you the most?

_____

_____

_____

_____

How can this reflection enhance your spiritual life?

_____

_____

_____

_____

What would you say to Jesus today?

_____

_____

_____

_____

"Therefore, whoever hears these words of mine and puts them into practice is like a wise man who built his house on the rock. The rain came down, the streams rose, and the winds blew and beat against that house; yet it did not fall, because it had its foundation on the rock."
Matthew 7:24-25

LAZARUS

The end did not want to wait; if it had waited a little longer, everything would have been different, they said. However, it hurried and took with it a friend, a brother. The farewell was incomplete; friends were missing, the almost brother was absent. One day he waited, two days he endured, but on the third, he left. The reunion would happen, he knew, for there is hope after death, he just didn't imagine it would be on the fourth day. In the silence of the cave, a voice echoed; this voice called him, woke him, and restored him. He had never seen so many astonished and admiring gazes, but among them all, it was the gaze of the Lord that reached him. Everyone thought it was the end, but how can the friend of Life die?

A man named Lazarus was sick. He was from the village of Bethany, where Mary and her sister Martha lived. The two sisters sent word to Jesus:
— Lord, your dear friend Lazarus is sick!
When Jesus received the news, He said:
— This sickness will not end in death. It is for God's glory so that God's Son may be glorified through it.
Jesus loved Martha, her sister, and Lazarus. However, when He heard that Lazarus was sick, He stayed where He was for two more days. Then He said to His disciples:
— Let us go back to Judea.
But they said:
— Rabbi, the Jews tried to stone You recently, and You are going back there?
Jesus answered:
— Are there not twelve hours of daylight? Anyone who walks in the daytime will not stumble, for they see by this world's light. It is when a person walks at night that they stumble, for they have no light.
After He said this, He went on to tell them:

— Our friend Lazarus has fallen asleep, but I am going there to wake him up.

His disciples replied:

— Lord, if he sleeps, he will get better.

Jesus had been speaking of his death, but His disciples thought He meant natural sleep. So then He told them plainly:

— Lazarus is dead, and for your sake I am glad I was not there, so that you may believe. But let us go to him.

Then Thomas (called Didymus) said to the rest of the disciples:

— Let us also go, that we may die with Him!

On His arrival, Jesus found that Lazarus had already been in the tomb for four days. Bethany was less than two miles from Jerusalem, and many Jews had come to Martha and Mary to comfort them in the loss of their brother. When Martha heard that Jesus was coming, she went out to meet Him, but Mary stayed at home.

Lord, Martha said to Jesus,

— If You had been here, my brother would not have died. But I know that even now God will give You whatever You ask.

Jesus said to her:

— Your brother will rise again.

Martha answered:

— I know he will rise again in the resurrection at the last day.

Jesus said to her:

— I am the resurrection and the life. The one who believes in Me will live, even though they die; and whoever lives by believing in Me will never die. Do you believe this?

— Yes, Lord, she replied. I believe that You are the Messiah, the Son of God, who is to come into the world.

After she had said this, she went back and called her sister Mary aside.

— The Teacher is here, she said, and is asking for you.

When Mary heard this, she got up quickly and went to Him. Now Jesus had not yet entered the village, but was still at the place where Martha had met Him. When the Jews who had been with

Mary in the house, comforting her, noticed how quickly she got up and went out, they followed her, supposing she was going to the tomb to mourn there.

When Mary reached the place where Jesus was and saw Him, she fell at His feet and said:

— Lord, if You had been here, my brother would not have died.

When Jesus saw her weeping, and the Jews who had come along with her also weeping, He was deeply moved in spirit and troubled.

— Where have you laid him? He asked.

— Come and see, Lord, they replied.

Jesus wept.

Then the Jews said:

— See how He loved him!

But some of them said:

— Could not He who opened the eyes of the blind man have kept this man from dying?

Jesus, once more deeply moved, came to the tomb. It was a cave with a stone laid across the entrance.

— Take away the stone, He said.

But Lord, said Martha, the sister of the dead man, by this time there is a bad odor, for he has been there four days.

Then Jesus said:

— Did I not tell you that if you believe, you will see the glory of God?

So they took away the stone. Then Jesus looked up and said:

— Father, I thank You that You have heard Me. I knew that You always hear Me, but I said this for the benefit of the people standing here, that they may believe that You sent Me.

When He had said this, Jesus called in a loud voice:

— Lazarus, come out!

The dead man came out, his hands and feet wrapped with strips of linen, and a cloth around his face.

Jesus said to them:

— Take off the grave clothes and let him go.

Therefore many of the Jews who had come to visit Mary, and had seen what Jesus did, believed in Him.

But some of them went to the Pharisees and told them what Jesus had done. Then the chief priests and the Pharisees called a meeting of the Sanhedrin.

— What are we accomplishing? they asked.

— Here is this man performing many signs. If we let him go on like this, everyone will believe in him, and then the Romans will come and take away both our temple and our nation.

Then one of them, named Caiaphas, who was high priest that year, spoke up:

— You know nothing at all!

— You do not realize that it is better for you that one man die for the people than that the whole nation perish.

He did not say this on his own, but as high priest that year he prophesied that Jesus would die for the Jewish nation, and not only for that nation but also for the scattered children of God, to bring them together and make them one.

So from that day on they plotted to take His life.

John 11:1-53

This miracle was only written by John, but it was not the first time Jesus raised someone from the dead. The first was the daughter of Jairus, the second was the widow of Nain's son, and now Lazarus. This miracle is so rich in details that we can divide it into four parts: Jesus' dialogue with the disciples, His interaction with Mary and Martha, the miracle itself, and the reaction of the religious leaders.

We can observe four conflicts in this miracle: the disciples did not understand the desire to return to a place of persecution; Martha and Mary could not comprehend the delay of the Master; Lazarus did not understand what had happened; and the Pharisees did not accept that Jesus was the Messiah. This shows us that God's plans are greater than any human understanding. Does the impossible really exist before a God who can do all things?

The Messenger

The text does not reveal the name or identity of this messenger. Because of the brief mention, "they sent word to Jesus," this character can easily go unnoticed. The distance he traveled was about 40 km. Given the importance of the task, he was certainly a trusted person. This messenger spoke with Jesus and likely heard the following declaration from the Master: "This illness will not end in death. It happened for the glory of God so that the Son of God may be glorified through it." Perhaps this was the message Jesus sent back to Mary and Martha.

There must have been great anticipation for the messenger's return with the Lord's message. Jesus entrusted this man with a prophecy of life, something that had not yet happened but that Jesus already saw as a done deal. I can imagine that this person must have shared this story for generations about the day he encountered the Messiah and heard the prophecy concerning Lazarus.

The Disciples

The disciples were the first to misunderstand God's purpose, even though Jesus explained everything in detail. It was as if their understanding was veiled, to the point that Jesus had to say: "This is for you to believe." They not only did not understand but also did not believe. They feared the persecution they had previously faced in the same town, yet they obeyed the Master's decision to return there. By witnessing Lazarus' resurrection, the disciples experienced Jesus' divine power over death. This miracle undoubtedly strengthened their faith and further confirmed Jesus' identity as the Messiah, although full understanding would only come with Jesus' own resurrection.

The Sisters

Certainly, Mary and Martha had prepared many meals for Jesus during His time of friendship with them. Jesus considered them friends, and the feeling was mutual. Their trust was placed in the Jesus who was a friend, not in the Jesus who was the Messiah, because of the intimacy they shared. The last thing they would have expected was for their friend to delay His arrival. They had seen Jesus perform miracles and knew He had the power to heal, but they did not understand that raising someone after four days was possible for the Master. They believed in the resurrection on the last day and believed Jesus was the Messiah, but they did not comprehend that Jesus was the resurrection and the life.

How many times must they have talked with Jesus about the miracles performed in the neighborhood? Jesus wept at the pain of Mary and Martha, showing His compassion. He knew He would raise Lazarus, but He was still moved by their suffering. This teaches us that God cares about our pain, even though He knows that, in the end, everything will be resolved.

The Friend

"The one you love, Lazarus, is sick," said the messenger. That would be enough for anyone to stop everything and rush to the friend's side. However, Jesus had another plan for Lazarus that no one could understand. None of the characters in this miracle could see that Lazarus' death had a predetermined purpose. Everyone saw a tragedy, but Jesus saw a purpose.

Lazarus did not need to believe or ask for help from the Lord, but while he "slept," Jesus worked on his behalf. As friends, they must have had many things in common, for Jesus considered him a friend. However, this friendship did not preserve him from the affliction of death, but the important thing is that he had Jesus as his resurrection and life. After his resurrection, Lazarus also became a target of persecution by the Pharisees. Many attribute the fact that only John narrated his story to the desire to protect him.

The Pharisees

This miracle was crucial in the Pharisees' decision to kill Jesus. They not only planned His death but also Lazarus', because they wanted to erase any evidence of Christ's power. It's sad to see that many, even after witnessing God's miracles in their lives, still do not understand that there is a Creator working on their behalf. The Pharisees saw Jesus' miracles, and yet they failed to understand that such wondrous works could only happen with God's participation.

❖

Days passed, and with them, all hope faded. "If only the Savior had come to save us, our brother would still be here," they said. Along the way, the Master's company marched toward the miracle. It could have been the company of faith, but without its leader, it seemed more like the company of uncertainty and fear. As they approached the village, those men did not know what they would find, but the Master knew what He would accomplish.

"Martha, your brother will rise again," He said. "I know, Lord," she replied, but in truth, she understood nothing. When Mary came, she poured out all her suffering at His feet, and though He was Lord, His heart was made of flesh. In His eyes, they finally found tears. Being God, He wept as a man; being a man, He loved as God. Between the miracle and Lazarus, there was a stone. Locked in a cave without an exit, it was no obstacle for the voice that carried life. The bandages tightened around his body, but they did not prevent him from following the call: "Lazarus, come out!" This was a voice he knew well; it was the voice of love calling him to a life embrace.

On that day, that people came to know the Messiah, who can call from death to life and give anyone the gift of life. He demonstrated that our faith—or lack of it—does not affect His plans or purposes.

What stood out to you the most?

_____

_____

_____

_____

_____

How can this reflection enhance your spiritual life?

_____

_____

_____

_____

_____

What would you say to Jesus today?

_____

_____

_____

_____

_____

*"Jesus said to her, 'I am the resurrection and the life.
He who believes in Me, though he may die, he shall live.
And whoever lives and believes in Me shall
never die. Do you believe this?'"*
John 11:25-26

BARTIMAEUS

It was a day like any other. To the sound of the wind, he listened to the birds, the pedestrians, and their footsteps. If it was a good day, he would hear the sound of coins falling into his cup. Suddenly, the ground began to shake; it was the sound of a crowd approaching. The crowd grew, and with every moment, it came closer. The noise intensified, and with it, his curiosity about so much commotion. "What's happening?" he asked. "The Prophet from Nazareth, Jesus, is passing by!" they replied. Then the son of Timaeus cried out to the Son of David, shouted as if there were no tomorrow, for that would be the day of his miracle.

Jesus and the disciples arrived at the city of Jericho. As he was leaving the city with the disciples and a large crowd, he met a blind man named Bartimaeus, son of Timaeus. The blind man was sitting by the roadside, begging. When he heard someone say that it was Jesus of Nazareth passing by, the blind man began to shout:
— Jesus, Son of David, have mercy on me!
Many people scolded him and told him to be quiet, but he shouted even louder:
— Son of David, have mercy on me!
Then Jesus stopped and said:
— Call the blind man.
They called him and said:
— Take courage! Get up because he is calling you!
Then Bartimaeus threw his cloak aside, stood up quickly, and went to where Jesus was.
— What do you want me to do for you? — Jesus asked.
— Master, I want to see again! — he replied.
— Go; you are healed because you had faith! — Jesus said.
At that very moment, Bartimaeus began to see again and followed Jesus along the road. Mark 10:46

Bartimaeus left behind three things he possessed: his cloak, his safe place, and his alms. To receive his miracle, he faced three obstacles: the crowd, fear, and uncertainty. Perhaps Jesus passed by several blind people along the way who were silenced by the same crowd because they did not have Bartimaeus's persistence. The blind were despised by the population, and a blind man shouting was a disturbance to the peace. However, Bartimaeus did not allow anyone to silence him.

Alone, with only his voice and resilience, he overcame a crowd. The more they asked him to be quiet, the louder he cried out. His voice was full of pain and desperation as he said, "Have mercy on me!" He knew that this could be his only chance to meet the Master. Could a cry change a man's life forever?

The crowd

As soon as he raised his voice crying out to Jesus, he began to receive opposition from the crowd. This was the first difficulty he had to overcome. The people who could have helped him became his greatest obstacle. His cry was the only weapon he had to fight, but it was enough to draw Jesus's attention. His shout was a broken cry, yet full of faith. Jesus could not resist these elements, and the expression of his pain attracted the Savior.

Fear

As a blind man and a beggar, Bartimaeus was despised by society. He had to overcome any feelings of unworthiness and fear in order to seek his healing. His condition of shame and rejection did not stop him from fighting for his miracle. The testimony about Jesus that he heard created in his heart a vision of the impossible. He believed that Jesus had mercy for him.

Uncertainty

Faced with the opposition of people and uncertainty about how he would be received, he needed courage to keep crying out to Jesus. He had no guarantee that Jesus would hear him or respond, but even so, he persevered. Even without the blessing in his hands, Bartimaeus left an example of resilience that inspires us to keep crying out until we achieve victory.

The familiar environment

The blind usually remained in the same place, often at the gates of temples or in public spaces, which increased their chances of receiving some alms. Staying in the same place also offered safety to the blind man.

When Bartimaeus heard that Jesus was calling him, he did not hesitate and immediately left his safe place and faced the challenge of a new place, one that could bring him what he so deeply desired.

The cloak

Bartimaeus's cloak represented his identity as a beggar; it marked his dependence on alms to survive. Moreover, it was an item of protection and security within his reality. When he left it behind upon being called by Jesus, he showed faith and determination, giving up his old life to receive healing and a new beginning. That cloak could only bring him alms, but the miracle would change his story. He did not come before Jesus carrying the reference of his past or his condition, but came uncovered, ready to receive garments of honor and a new life.

The alms

All he had was his daily portion of alms. Through them, he could survive until the next day. When he left everything behind, it was as if he was saying that his comfort zone, the protection of his cloak, and any alms he had at the moment were no longer more important than an encounter with Jesus.

Imagine if he had not received healing: he would have had to ask someone to take him back to his old spot, bring back his cloak, and hope that his alms had not been stolen. Yet, that did not happen, because his faith was placed in Jesus.

When we go through difficulties, nothing changes until we shift our position. The same happened with this blind man. Jesus was walking along the road, and nothing happened until the moment he cried out. When he shouted, "Jesus, Son of David, have mercy on me!" he triggered a response from the Lord. Many tried to silence him, but he insisted, crying even louder, and for this attitude he was rewarded.

Isn't it the same with us? Sometimes we suffer in silence until we reach the point where we can no longer bear it and cry out, "God, help me! Jesus, rescue me!" Bartimaeus had faith, because Jesus said: "Your faith has saved you." Your faith can heal and can also solve any of your problems.

God asks us today: "What do you want Me to do for you?" If we do not cry out, He will continue to look at us, waiting until, by faith, we provoke His reaction. When we ask with faith, God responds, because He always hears us. God does not despise a contrite heart. He says: "You will seek me and find me when you seek me with all your heart." Jeremiah 29:13

The Lord's goodness is infinite and accessible to all, but our posture before Him makes all the difference. There is restoration for your life, there is relief for your pain and a solution for your problems. However, it is necessary to cry out, persist, and provoke a response. God seeks a contrite heart and a soul open to receive Him with faith, like the faith of the blind man from Jericho.

Where is your faith? Is it in your comfort zone, in the protection of a cloak, or in the strength of your own arm? Where have you placed your faith? Place your trust in Jesus, just as the blind man from Jericho did. He received his blessing, his restoration, and his salvation. His life was transformed because he trusted in the power of Jesus. If we place our faith in God, we will never be ashamed—never! It is impossible to be abandoned when our faith is rooted in Christ.

What stood out to you the most?

_____

_____

_____

_____

_____

How can this reflection enhance your spiritual life?

_____

_____

_____

_____

_____

What would you say to Jesus today?

_____

_____

_____

_____

_____

_____

"Then Jesus cried out and said, 'He who believes in Me, believes not in Me but in Him who sent Me. And he who sees Me sees Him who sent Me. I have come as a light into the world, that whoever believes in Me should not abide in darkness.'"

John 12:44-46

THE BARREN FIG TREE

It should have been an ordinary journey between two cities, but between them there was a tree. It was not the tree of life, nor the tree of the knowledge of good and evil. So, what caught the Master's attention about it? The Bread of Life desired earthly food; the One who fed multitudes found nothing on it that could be multiplied, but He used it as an opportunity to teach.

Jesus entered Jerusalem, went to the Temple, and looked around at everything. But as it was already late, He went to the village of Bethany with the twelve disciples. The next day, as they were returning from Bethany, Jesus felt hungry. He saw a fig tree in the distance, full of leaves, and went to see if there were any figs on it. When He got closer, He found only leaves, because it was not the season for figs. Then He said to the fig tree,
— May no one ever eat your fruit again! And His disciples heard this. The next day, early in the morning, Jesus and the disciples passed by the fig tree and saw that it had withered from the roots. Then Peter remembered what had happened and said to Jesus,
— Look, Master! The fig tree that You cursed has withered.
Jesus answered,
— Have faith in God, because truly I tell you, anyone who says to this mountain, 'Be lifted up and thrown into the sea,' and does not doubt in his heart, but believes that what he says will happen, it will be done for him.

Therefore, I tell you, whatever you ask for in prayer, believe that you have received it, and it will be yours. And when you stand praying, if you hold anything against anyone, forgive him, so that your Father in heaven may forgive you your sins. But if you do not forgive, neither will your Father in heaven forgive your sins. Mark 11:11-26

Some interpret the miracle of the fruitless fig tree as a symbol of Israel and Judaism, a call for repentance and fruitfulness, a warning against sterile religion as well as false appearances of fruitfulness. However, the direct example that Jesus teaches in this episode is directly related to faith.

This miracle is unique in many aspects. Jesus had already performed miracles involving various natural elements, such as water, wind, storms, loaves, and fish, but this time He interacted with a fruit tree—actually, a fruitless one. The text says that Jesus, seeing from a distance a fig tree full of leaves, went to see if He might find anything on it and, upon approaching, found nothing but leaves, because it was not the season for figs.

I have always questioned why Jesus had to curse the fig tree if it was not the season for figs. After researching, I understood that the fig tree, when full of leaves, already signals the presence of figs. So, when Jesus saw the fig tree with leaves from a distance, He went to look for fruit, but found nothing but leaves.

Jesus spoke to the fig tree in the morning; then He went to the temple, and when they returned along the same path, Peter saw that the fig tree had dried up from the roots and alerted Jesus about what had happened. Then, He explained to Peter and the disciples the conditions for a miracle. He taught that, for a miracle to happen, there could be no doubt in the heart. We understand why His miracles happened quickly and always succeeded: He did not doubt in His spirit, for He had unwavering faith and did not carry any doubt in His heart.

He taught that everything is possible for those who ask in faith, without doubting. He explained to Peter and the disciples how this works. Peter says: "Master, the fig tree You cursed has withered." And Jesus replied: "Have faith in God." This was the first step. The second step was the declaration of faith in what is desired: "whoever says." The third step was to believe that it will happen exactly as it was spoken: "and does not doubt in his heart

168

but believes that what he says will be done, it will be done for him." The fourth step was being at peace with God and with the brother. He explained: "forgive if you have anything against anyone."

All these conditions work together. If we were to paraphrase these four verses in one, we would say: "Whoever speaks without doubting can have everything they desire, as long as they are at peace with their brother and with God." Those men had the privilege of learning how to decode how to achieve a miracle. Until then, they did not know how Jesus operated and, even less, did they know that everything He did was based on faith and love. Jesus had to make it clear many times that they were capable of doing the same and even greater things, using His power and authority according to the Father's will.

In this miracle, Jesus teaches how to achieve any miracle, a lesson that every Christian should always follow. When we reach moments of indignation in life, when our patience with difficulty reaches its limit, it is at this moment that this prayer should be made. When you can't take a situation anymore, use the same words that Jesus used: "Never again!" Jesus said to that fig tree: "May no one ever eat of your fruits again!" It was as if He were telling that tree that His patience had ended and that He would not allow that situation to repeat.

There are situations in life that require this spiritual command, this indignation, to say: "Never again!" "Never again sickness!" "Never again torment!" "Never again lack!" What is the "never again" in your life?

Our condition will always be determined by our position; where we live, how we live, our profession, our relationships. We endure many bad conditions simply for convenience and lack of attitude. If we learn from Jesus, whenever any condition is not what God has planned for us, our prayer must be: "Never again!"

What stood out to you the most?

_____

_____

_____

_____

_____

How can this reflection enhance your spiritual life?

_____

_____

_____

_____

What would you say to Jesus today?

_____

_____

_____

_____

*"But the natural man does not receive the things of the
Spirit of God, for they are foolishness to him; nor can he know
them, because they are spiritually discerned. But he who is
spiritual judges all things, yet he himself is rightly judged by no
one. For who has known the mind of the Lord that he may
instruct Him? But we have the mind of Christ."*
I Corinthians 2:14-16

PETER AND MALCHUS

That night, He was walking with His lamp toward Gethsemane. He had no idea that His life would change completely and that His plans for capture would be transformed. Unexpectedly, He felt the blade tear into His flesh, the burning pain mixing with astonishment. A servant, amidst the chaos, did not expect mercy, but found the hand that heals instead of the one that wounds. The moment His ear was restored, the echo of love spoke louder than the sword. There, before the accused, He saw the power that does not destroy, but restores.

When Jesus had said these things, He went out with His disciples across the Kidron Valley, where there was a garden, which He and His disciples entered. And Judas, who was betraying Him, also knew the place, because Jesus often met there with His disciples. So, having received the detachment of soldiers and officers from the chief priests and Pharisees, Judas came there with lanterns, torches, and weapons. Knowing all that was going to happen to Him, Jesus went out and asked them, "Who is it you want?"

"Jesus of Nazareth," they replied.

"I am He," Jesus said. And Judas, the traitor, was standing there with them. When Jesus said, "I am He," they drew back and fell to the ground.

Again He asked them, "Who is it you want?"

And they said, "Jesus of Nazareth."

"I told you that I am He," Jesus answered. "If you are looking for Me, then let these men go." This happened so that the words He had spoken would be fulfilled: "I have not lost one of those You gave Me."

Then Simon Peter, who had a sword, drew it and struck the high priest's servant, cutting off his right ear. The servant's name was Malchus. Jesus commanded Peter, "Put your sword away! Shall I not drink the cup the Father has given Me?"

Then the detachment of soldiers with its commander and the Jewish officials arrested Jesus. They bound Him and brought Him first to Annas, who was the father-in-law of Caiaphas, the high priest that year. John 18:1-10, Luke 22:51-53

The name Malchus (Μάλχος, Malchos in Greek) means "king." Therefore, the name Malchus may have been a prestigious name, although he was a servant, as the text states he was a servant of the High Priest. Jesus' arrest was essentially a religious mission, as it was ordered by the Sanhedrin, which was the Jewish council responsible for religious and legal matters at the time.

The religious leaders saw Jesus as a threat to their authority and to the stability of the temple. The temple guards and the Roman guard also watched from a distance, but Malchus was not part of these groups. He was the right-hand man of the High Priest Annas. Given the importance of Jesus' arrest, it is clear that Malchus was in line for the high priesthood.

The High Priest, as the highest authority, would be something like a Catholic Pope today. Malchus was his trusted man. Jesus' arrest was such an important event for the religious leaders that, after the miracle of Lazarus' resurrection, they said: "We are going to lose everything, because if this man keeps performing miracles, the Romans will come, take the synagogue, take our king, take everything, and we will be left with nothing." For this reason, the High Priest put Malchus in charge of this mission. Malchus was leading them, and when Simon Peter drew his sword, he struck exactly the one who was in charge.

An interesting thing about this event is that everyone was shocked by Peter's action and did not react immediately. This gave Jesus time to calm everyone, say "enough," and put Malchus' ear back in place. They did not expect violence from Jesus. Surely, Judas had said: "Don't worry, the Master preaches love. He has never used violence with anyone. He only preaches peace. There will be no problem, and it will be easy to arrest Him. He is in Gethsemane, in the Garden of Olives." When Peter used the sword, everyone was surprised because Jesus was not a violent man, but He quickly corrected everything, rebuked Peter, restored, and healed.

Malchus left home to fulfill a mission. He did not need a miracle and did not know he would receive one. However, he was the one who received the miracle the fastest. As soon as he needed it, Jesus healed him. If Malchus had remained without his ear, he would have been considered defective and could never be a priest or offer sacrifices in the temple. He would suffer prejudice and lose his position as the servant of the High Priest. The moment the sword cut his ear, his life seemed to be over because a person with a physical defect could not serve in the temple. He was probably already in the priesthood school and was helping the High Priest, aiming to one day occupy that position. However, if he remained with a defect, he would never reach there.

Imagine Malchus explaining to his wife why his clothes were stained with blood if he had no other wounds on his body. Each time someone asked him about the incident, he was forced to testify about the goodness of Jesus and His healing power.

Another important aspect in this text is the demonstration of Jesus' unconditional love. The Bible says there is no greater love than one who gives his life for his friends. Jesus did not just give His life for His friends, but for all humanity. He acted in love, being the personification of God's love. At the moment of His arrest, His first concern was to protect His disciples: "You can arrest Me, but let these men go." His second concern was to heal Malchus.

Being the right-hand man of the High Priest, he witnessed all the discussions between Jesus and the religious leaders of the time. He knew all His miracles, teachings, and signs. Could it be that, after the healing and restoration he received from Jesus, he changed his opinion? Perhaps everything he thought about the Lord changed because he had a personal encounter with the Messiah.

I imagine people asking him afterward: "Is it true that you lost your ear, and Jesus healed you?" Now, he would have to declare the power and mercy of Jesus. I always say that it is impossible to encounter Jesus and leave the same. Malchus had everything planned for that day. He probably planned the arrest, the dialogues, everything he would say, but everything changed when he encountered Jesus. His plans were transformed by this encounter. His perspective changed. His opinions changed. And, by Jesus' mercy, he received his miracle.

He did not leave home like many others to go to the synagogue hoping to see Jesus and witness a miracle. On the contrary, he went to arrest Him. What do you think he understood after this event? Maybe he pondered: "I arrested the man who healed me and was part of His death." Of course, the true responsible was the High Priest, who gave the order, but he was an instrument. The Bible does not report what happened to Malchus; however, I can imagine him believing in Jesus as Savior shortly after the Resurrection.

At Jesus' Resurrection, the guards at the tomb witnessed God's power and the miracle of the Resurrection. They saw the angel, the earthquake, and the stone removed. However, the religious leaders said: "We will pay you to say that the disciples stole the body." Malchus certainly knew about this. Now, he knew that Jesus healed, that He was good, and that He fulfilled exactly what He promised: to rise.

Malchus did not seek, did not believe, did not deserve, but received his miracle. So, you who believe, who have a covenant with God, who seek Him and have faith—will you not receive? Of course, you will! Maybe not in the time you imagine, but if we persevere, we will receive. If Jesus had mercy on Malchus, in the same way, He will have mercy on our needs, for God does not show favoritism according to His promises. "He who did not spare His own Son, but gave Him up for us all, how will He not also, along with Him, graciously give us all things?" Romans 8:32

What stood out to you the most?

_____

_____

_____

_____

How can this reflection enhance your spiritual life?

_____

_____

_____

_____

What would you say to Jesus today?

_____

_____

_____

_____

_____

"This was His eternal purpose, which He accomplished in Christ Jesus our Lord. Through faith in Christ, we now have boldness and confidence to access the presence of God."
Ephesians 3:11-12

THE CRUCIFIXION

The hour had come, and He who was offered before the foundation of the world was walking toward His destiny. His steps raised the dust of the earth, while the fury of His enemies spilled His pure blood onto the ground. Along the way, the marks of His holiness were left, while the earth was moistened with the sweat of His sacrifice. With each passing moment, the weight only grew, and it seemed as though the burden of all humanity was upon His shoulders.

Those who followed the scene of cruelty did not imagine that the weight of their own wrongs was being carried by Him. The Blessed One made Himself accursed so that all might be made sons. As He was lifted up, He raised with Him all the fallen, and to the captives, He set them all free at once. As His flesh was torn, a new and living way was opened, by which we can reach the top of heaven. In His final cry, He divided eternity into two paths: one of salvation and the other of eternal forgetfulness.

Jesus before Pilate (Jn 18:28, Lk 23:2, Jn 18:31)

They led Jesus therefore from Caiaphas into the Praetorium. It was early, and they themselves didn't enter into the Praetorium, that they might not be defiled, but might eat the Passover. Pilate therefore went out to them, and said, "What accusation do you bring against this man?"

They answered him, "If this man weren't an evildoer, we wouldn't have delivered him up to you." They began to accuse him, saying, "We found this man perverting the nation, forbidding paying taxes to Caesar, and saying that he himself is Christ, a king." Pilate therefore said to them, "Take him yourselves, and judge him according to your law." Therefore, the Jews said to him, "It is illegal for us to put anyone to death," that the word of Jesus might be fulfilled, which he spoke, signifying by what kind of death he should die.

Pilate interrogates Jesus *(Jn 18:33)*

Pilate therefore entered again into the Praetorium, called Jesus, and said to him, "Are you the King of the Jews?" Jesus answered him, "Do you say this by yourself, or did others tell you about me?" Pilate answered, "I'm not a Jew, am I? Your own nation and the chief priests delivered you to me. What have you done?" Jesus answered, "My Kingdom is not of this world. If my Kingdom were of this world, then my servants would fight, that I wouldn't be delivered to the Jews. But now my Kingdom is not from here."

Pilate deliberates *(Jo 18:37, Mt 27:12)*

Pilate therefore said to him, "Are you a king then?" Jesus answered, "You say that I am a king. For this reason, I have been born, and for this reason I have come into the world, that I should testify to the truth. Everyone who is of the truth listens to my voice." Pilate said to him, "What is truth?" When he had said this, he went out again to the Jews, and said to them, "I find no basis for a charge against him. But you have a custom, that I should release someone to you at the Passover. Therefore, do you want me to release to you the King of the Jews?" Then they all shouted again, saying, "Not this man, but Barabbas!" Now Barabbas was a robber. When he was accused by the chief priests and elders, he answered nothing. Then Pilate said to him, "Don't you hear how many things they testify against you?" He gave him no answer, not even one word, so that the governor marveled greatly.

Jesus before Herod *(Lk 23:5)*

But they insisted, saying, "He stirs up the people, teaching throughout all Judea, beginning from Galilee even to this place." But when Pilate heard Galilee mentioned, he asked if the man was a Galilean. When he found out that he was in Herod's jurisdiction, he sent him to Herod, who was also in Jerusalem during those days. Now when Herod saw Jesus, he was exceedingly glad, for he had wanted to see him for a long time, because he had heard many things about him. He hoped to see some miracle done by him. He questioned him with many words, but he gave no answers. The chief priests and the scribes stood, vehemently accusing him. Herod with his soldiers humiliated him and mocked him. Dressing him in luxurious clothing, they sent him back to Pilate. Herod and Pilate became friends with each other that very day, for before that they were enemies with each other.

Pilate's wife (Mt 27:19)

While he was sitting on the judgment seat, his wife sent to him, saying, "Have nothing to do with that righteous man, for I have suffered many things today in a dream because of him."

Pilate does not find fault in Jesus (Lk 23:13)

Pilate called together the chief priests, the rulers, and the people, and said to them, "You brought this man to me as one that perverts the people, and behold, having examined him before you, I found no basis for a charge against this man concerning those things of which you accuse him. Neither has Herod, for I sent you to him, and see, nothing worthy of death has been done by him. I will therefore chastise him and release him."

Jesus or Barabbas (Mk 15:6)

Now at the feast he used to release to them one prisoner, whom they asked of him. There was one called Barabbas, bound with his fellow insurgents, men who in the insurrection had committed murder. The multitude, crying aloud, began to ask him to do as he always did for them. Pilate answered them, saying, "Do you want me to release to you the King of the Jews?" For he perceived that for envy the chief priests had delivered him up. But the chief priests stirred up the multitude, that he should release Barabbas to them instead. Pilate again asked them, "What then should I do to him whom you call the King of the Jews?" They cried out again, "Crucify him!" Pilate said to them, "Why, what evil has he done?" But they cried out exceedingly, "Crucify him!" Pilate, wishing to please the multitude, released Barabbas to them, and handed over Jesus, when he had flogged him, to be crucified.

The Crown of Thorns *(Mt 27:27)*

Then the governor's soldiers took Jesus into the Praetorium, and gathered the whole garrison together against him. They stripped him and put a scarlet robe on him. They braided a crown of thorns and put it on his head, and a reed in his right hand; and they kneeled down before him and mocked him, saying, "Hail, King of the Jews!" They spat on him, and took the reed and struck him on the head.

Pilate tries to release Jesus (Jn 19:4)

Then Pilate went out again, and said to them, "Behold, I bring him out to you, that you may know that I find no basis for a charge against him." Jesus therefore came out, wearing the crown of thorns and the purple garment. Pilate said to them, "Behold, the man!" When therefore the chief priests and the officers saw him, they shouted, saying, "Crucify! Crucify!" Pilate said to them, "Take him yourselves, and crucify him, for I find no basis for a charge against him." The Jews answered him, "We have a law, and by our law he ought to die, because he made himself the Son of God." When therefore Pilate heard this saying, he was more afraid. He entered into the Praetorium again, and said to Jesus, "Where are you from?" But Jesus gave him no answer. Pilate therefore said to him, "Aren't you speaking to me? Don't you know that I have power to release you and have power to crucify you?" Jesus answered, "You would have no power at all against me, unless it were given to you from above. Therefore, he who delivered me to you has greater sin." At this, Pilate was seeking to release him, but the Jews cried out, saying, "If you release this man, you aren't Caesar's friend! Everyone who makes himself a king speaks against Caesar!" When Pilate therefore heard these words, he brought Jesus out and sat down on the judgment seat at a place called "The Pavement", but in Hebrew, "Gabbatha." Now it was the Preparation Day of the Passover, at about the sixth hour. He said to the Jews, "Behold, your King!" They cried out, "Away with him! Away with him! Crucify him!" Pilate said to them,

"Shall I crucify your King?" The chief priests answered, "We have no king but Caesar!"

Pilate washes his hands *(Mt 27:24)*

So, when Pilate saw that nothing was being gained, but rather that a disturbance was starting, he took water and washed his hands before the multitude, saying, "I am innocent of the blood of this righteous person. You see to it." All the people answered, "May his blood be on us and on our children!"

They release Barabbas *(Lk 23:24)*

Pilate decreed that what they asked for should be done. He released him who had been thrown into prison for insurrection and murder, for whom they asked, but he delivered Jesus up to their will.

Jesus is taken to the crucifixion *(Mk 15:20, Jn 19:17)*

When they had mocked him, they took the purple off him, and put his own garments on him. They led him out to crucify him. He went out, bearing his cross, to the place called "The Place of a Skull", which is called in Hebrew, "Golgotha"

Women cry for Jesus *(Lk 23:27)*

A great multitude of the people followed him, including women who also mourned and lamented him. But Jesus, turning to them, said, "Daughters of Jerusalem, don't weep for me, but weep for yourselves and for your children. For behold, the days are coming in which they will say, 'Blessed are the barren, the wombs that never bore, and the breasts that never nursed.' Then they will begin to tell the mountains, 'Fall on us!' and tell the hills, 'Cover us.' For if they do these things in the green tree, what will be done in the dry?"

The crucifixion *(Mt 27:33, Jn 19:23)*

When they came to a place called "Golgotha", that is to say, "The place of a skull," they gave him sour wine to drink mixed with gall. When he had tasted it, he would not drink. Then the soldiers, when they had crucified Jesus, took his garments and made four parts, to every soldier a part; and also, the coat. Now the coat was without seam, woven from the top throughout. Then they said to one another, "Let's not tear it, but cast lots for it to decide whose it will be," that the Scripture might be fulfilled, which says, "They parted my garments among them. For my cloak they cast lots.

Jesus intercedes for his enemies *(Lk 23:34)*

Jesus said, "Father, forgive them, for they don't know what they are doing."

The third hour *(Jn 19:19, Mk 15:25, Mt 27:43)*

Pilate wrote a title also, and put it on the cross. There was written, "*JESUS OF NAZARETH, THE KING OF THE JEWS.*" Therefore, many of the Jews read this title, for the place where Jesus was crucified was near the city; and it was written in Hebrew, in Latin, and in Greek.

The chief priests of the Jews therefore said to Pilate, "Don't write, 'The King of the Jews,' but, 'he said, "I am King of the Jews."'" Pilate answered, "What I have written, I have written." It was the third hour, and they crucified him. The superscription of his accusation was written over him, "*THE KING OF THE JEWS.*" With him they crucified two robbers; one on his right hand, and one on his left. The Scripture was fulfilled, which says, "He was counted with transgressors." Those who passed by blasphemed him, wagging their heads, and saying, "Ha! You who destroy the temple, and build it in three days, save yourself, and come down from the cross!" Likewise, also the chief priests mocking among themselves with the scribes said, "He saved others. He can't save himself. Let the Christ, the King of Israel, now come down from the cross, that we may see and believe him." Those who were crucified with him also insulted him. He trusts in God. Let God deliver him now, if he wants him; for he said, 'I am the Son of God.'"

Mocked by soldiers *(Lk 23:36)*

The soldiers also mocked him, coming to him and offering him vinegar, and saying, "If you are the King of the Jews, save yourself!"

Today you will be with me in paradise (Lk 23:39)

One of the criminals who was hanged insulted him, saying, "If you are the Christ, save yourself and us!" But the other answered, and rebuking him said, "Don't you even fear God, seeing you are under the same condemnation? And we indeed justly, for we receive the due reward for our deeds, but this man has done nothing wrong." He said to Jesus, "Lord, remember me when you come into your Kingdom." Jesus said to him, "Assuredly I tell you, today you will be with me in Paradise."

Jesus asks John for Mary (Jn 19:25)

But standing by Jesus' cross were his mother, his mother's sister, Mary the wife of Clopas, and Mary Magdalene. Therefore, when Jesus saw his mother, and the disciple whom he loved standing there, he said to his mother, "Woman, behold, your son!" Then he said to the disciple, "Behold, your mother!" From that hour, the disciple took her to his own home.

The sixth hour: Darkness on earth (Mt 27:45)

Now from the sixth hour there was darkness over all the land until the ninth hour.

The ninth hour: My God, my God! (Mt 27:46, Mt27:49)

About the ninth hour Jesus cried with a loud voice, saying, "Eli, Eli, lima sabachthani?" That is, "My God, my God, why have you forsaken me?" Some of them who stood there, when they heard it, said, "This man is calling Elijah." The rest said, "Let him be. Let's see whether Elijah comes to save him."

Jesus' death (Jn 19:28, Lk 23:46, Jn 19:30b, Lk 23:48)

After this, Jesus, seeing that all things were now finished, that the Scripture might be fulfilled, said, "I am thirsty." Now a vessel full of vinegar was set there; so, they put a sponge full of the vinegar on hyssop, and held it at his mouth. When Jesus therefore had received the vinegar, he said, "It is finished." Jesus, crying with a loud voice, said, "Father, into your hands I commit my spirit!" Having said this, he breathed his last. ... Jesus, crying with a loud voice, said, "Father, into your hands I commit my spirit!"

Having said this, he breathed his last. All the multitudes that came together to see this, when they saw the things that were done, returned home beating their breasts. All his acquaintances and the women who followed with him from Galilee stood at a distance, watching these things.

The veil of the temple tears (Mt 27:51)

Behold, the veil of the temple was torn in two from the top to the bottom. The earth quaked and the rocks were split. The tombs were opened, and many bodies of the saints who had fallen asleep were raised; and coming out of the tombs after his resurrection, they entered into the holy city and appeared to many.

The centurion believes (Mt 27:54)

Now the centurion and those who were with him watching Jesus, when they saw the earthquake and the things that were done, were terrified, saying, "Truly this was the Son of God!" Many women were there watching from afar, who had followed Jesus from Galilee, serving him. Among them were Mary Magdalene, Mary the mother of James and Joseph, and the mother of the sons of Zebedee.

Jesus pierced (Jn 19:31)

Therefore, the Jews, because it was the Preparation Day, so that the bodies wouldn't remain on the cross on the Sabbath (for that Sabbath was a special one), asked of Pilate that their legs might be broken, and that they might be taken away. Therefore, the soldiers came, and broke the legs of the first, and of the other who was crucified with him; but when they came to Jesus, and saw that he was already dead, they didn't break his legs. However, one of the soldiers pierced his side with a spear, and immediately blood and water came out. He who has seen has testified, and his testimony is true. He knows that he tells the truth, that you may believe. For these things happened that the Scripture might be fulfilled, "A bone of him will not be broken." Again, another Scripture says, "They will look on him whom they pierced.

In His most difficult moment, His closest friends abandoned Him. He endured everything alone and, even though He had not sinned, He made Himself sin to save all humanity. His sacrifice opened a new and living way through His redeeming blood. The Holy One offered Himself for the lost in order to restore sons and daughters to God. The voluntary surrender of His life divided eternity into two parts, tearing the curtain that separated the Holy from the unholy. Now, access to God has become direct and effective through His name – Jesus.

The unique and eternal sacrifice of Jesus granted mankind access to the presence of God. No other person would be qualified to carry out this perfect and eternal sacrifice, and no other name is worthy of being praised or invoked for us to receive anything from God.

Many believe that Jesus' death was caused by His suffering on the cross. However, He declares that no one can take His life and that this is a command from the Father. In John 10:17-18, we read: "For this reason the Father loves me, because I lay down my life that I may take it up again. No one takes it from me, but I lay it down of my own accord. I have authority to lay it down and I have authority to take it up again. This command I received from my Father." We then understand that His death was a miracle.

We might think that Jesus was forced to the cross by the Roman soldiers, but He Himself declares that He could call upon the angels of heaven to help Him if He wished. We understand, therefore, that His entire path to death on the cross had already been determined by God. Supernatural signs occurred after His death, such as the darkness that covered the earth from noon to three in the afternoon. The veil of the temple, which separated the Holy of Holies, was torn from top to bottom, the earthquake, and the resurrection of many saints, showing that the death of Jesus brought life.

Mark 15:32 describes this scene, saying: "Those crucified with him also heaped insults on him." This reveals that both criminals were insulting Jesus, but it is interesting to note that, during the crucifixion, one of them understood that Jesus was who He claimed to be, repented and turned to the Master. How many signs do we need to see to believe that God loves us and has prepared a path for our salvation? The difference between the three characters is worth observing.

The criminal on the left decided to curse and insult the Lord, as if it were Jesus' fault that he was being crucified. Surely, we've seen people who never admit their mistakes. For them, it's always someone else's fault. These people live in pessimism and are always watching and pointing out the faults of others.

The centurion also couldn't see salvation in Jesus, even being so close to the Master and witnessing His final hours. Only after His death did he pay attention to the signs. These signs were so striking that the centurion believed. Upon seeing the phenomena, he recognized that Jesus was the Son of God, but we do not know if he was converted.

The repentant criminal, on the other hand, believed in Jesus even without seeing the signs and was saved. We will never know what exactly led this man to convert. Was it Jesus' calm and tranquility? Was it His authority in speech? Perhaps he heard the Lord's dialogues with Pilate and reflected on salvation. One thing is certain: he did not need to see the signs at Jesus' death. He did not wait for the earthquake or the darkness on the earth to believe. Jesus recognized his repentance and his genuine change of mind. How many people would like to hear from Jesus what that man heard?

What a change of attitude he had! Even in life's final moments, Jesus is still standing with open arms to receive us, forgive us and give us eternal life. As long as there is life, there is an open door, and that door is Jesus. However, the final moment is often quick and unpredictable. That is why today is the day of salvation, because tomorrow does not belong to us. If we believe in the Son of God as our one and only Savior, He will surely receive us!

What stood out to you the most?

_____

_____

_____

_____

_____

How can this reflection enhance your spiritual life?

_____

_____

_____

_____

_____

What would you say to Jesus today?

_____

_____

_____

_____

_____

_____

"I give them eternal life, and they shall never perish; no one can snatch them out of My hand. My Father, who has given them to Me, is greater than all; and no one can snatch them out of the Father's hand. I and the Father are one."

John 10:28-30

THE RESURRECTION AND THE FORTY DAYS

Darkness hovered over the earth, and the enemies of the Light celebrated their deeds, but between the darkness and the Light there was a promise – on the third day I will rise again! The Pharisees trusted in the soldiers, the soldiers trusted in the stone, but the Word brought life and resurrection. Could a word bring life back and move a heavy stone? What chance would someone who had succumbed to death have? It was not just any word, it was the Word of life who created the worlds and with His breath set the heavens in place. His strength has no limits, except those created by Himself. On the third day, the dark cave encountered the light that formed the world, and the heavy stone that blocked the entrance did not prevent the Savior from coming out. The human garments gave way to the garments of eternity, and where His body once lay, only memories remained. He lifted us up on the cross so that He could raise us to life together.

The stone removed (Mt 28:2)

Behold, there was a great earthquake, for an angel of the Lord descended from the sky and came and rolled away the stone from the door and sat on it. His appearance was like lightning, and his clothing white as snow. For fear of him, the guards shook, and became like dead men.

Women go to the tomb (Mk 16:1)

When the Sabbath was past, Mary Magdalene, and Mary the mother of James, and Salome, bought spices, that they might come and anoint him. Very early on the first day of the week, they came to the tomb when the sun had risen. They were saying among themselves, "Who will roll away the stone from the door of the tomb for us?" for it was very big. Looking up, they saw that the stone was rolled back.

Announced resurrection *(Mk 16:5, Mt 28:5, Lk 24:5b, Mt 28:7, Mk 16:8b)*

Entering into the tomb, they saw a young man sitting on the right side, dressed in a white robe, and they were amazed. He said to them, "Don't be amazed. You seek Jesus, the Nazarene, who has been crucified. He has risen. He is not here. Behold, the place where they laid him! But go, tell his disciples and Peter, 'He goes before you into Galilee. There you will see him, as he said to you.'" The angel answered the women, "Don't be afraid, for I know that you seek Jesus, who has been crucified. He is not here, for he has risen, just like he said. Come, see the place where the Lord was lying.... "Why do you seek the living among the dead? He isn't here, but is risen. Remember what he told you when he was still in Galilee, saying that the Son of Man must be delivered up into the hands of sinful men and be crucified, and the third day rise again?" They remembered his words...Go quickly and tell his disciples, 'He has risen from the dead, and behold, he goes before you into Galilee; there you will see him.' Behold, I have told you." They departed quickly from the tomb with fear and great joy, and ran to bring his disciples word. They said nothing to anyone; for they were afraid.

The guards notify the priests *(Mt 28:11)*

Now while they were going, behold, some of the guards came into the city and told the chief priests all the things that had happened. When they were assembled with the elders and had taken counsel, they gave a large amount of silver to the soldiers, saying, "Say that his disciples came by night and stole him away while we slept. If this comes to the governor's ears, we will persuade him and make you free of worry." So, they took the money and did as they were told. This saying was spread abroad among the Jews, and continues until today.

Peter and John are warned *(Jn 20:2)*

Therefore, she ran and came to Simon Peter and to the other disciple whom Jesus loved, and said to them, "They have taken away the Lord out of the tomb, and we don't know where they have laid him!"

Peter and John run to the tomb (Jn 20:3)

Therefore, Peter and the other disciple went out, and they went toward the tomb. They both ran together. The other disciple outran Peter, and came to the tomb first. Stooping and looking in, he saw the linen cloths lying, yet he didn't enter in. Then Simon Peter came, following him, and entered into the tomb. He saw the linen cloths lying, and the cloth that had been on his head, not lying with the linen cloths, but rolled up in a place by itself. So, then the other disciple who came first to the tomb also entered in, and he saw and believed. For as yet they didn't know the Scripture that he must rise from the dead. So, the disciples went away again to their own homes.

Jesus appears to Mary Magdalene (Mk 16:9, Jn 20:11, Mk 16:10)

Now when he had risen early on the first day of the week, he appeared first to Mary Magdalene, from whom he had cast out seven demons. But Mary was standing outside at the tomb weeping. So, as she wept, she stooped and looked into the tomb, and she saw two angels in white sitting, one at the head, and one at the feet, where the body of Jesus had lain. They asked her, "Woman, why are you weeping?" She said to them, "Because they have taken away my Lord, and I don't know where they have laid him." When she had said this, she turned around and saw Jesus standing, and didn't know that it was Jesus. Jesus said to her, "Woman, why are you weeping? Who are you looking for?" She, supposing him to be the gardener, said to him, "Sir, if you have carried him away, tell me where you have laid him, and I will take him away." Jesus said to her, "Mary." She turned and said to him, "Rabboni!" which is to say, "Teacher!" Jesus said to her, "Don't hold me, for I haven't yet ascended to my Father; but go to my brothers and tell them, 'I am ascending to my Father and your

189

Father, to my God and your God.'" She went and told those who had been with him, as they mourned and wept. When they heard that he was alive, and had been seen by her, they disbelieved.

Jesus appears to other women (Mt 28:9)

As they went to tell his disciples, behold, Jesus met them, saying, "Rejoice!" They came and took hold of his feet, and worshiped him. Then Jesus said to them, "Don't be afraid. Go tell my brothers that they should go into Galilee, and there they will see me."

The women report to the disciples (Lk 24:8)

They remembered his words, returned from the tomb, and told all these things to the eleven and to all the rest. Now they were Mary Magdalene, Joanna, and Mary the mother of James. The other women with them told these things to the apostles. These words seemed to them to be nonsense, and they didn't believe them.

Jesus appears to two disciples going to Emmaus (Lk 24:13)

Behold, two of them were going that very day to a village named Emmaus, which was sixty stadia from Jerusalem. They talked with each other about all of these things which had happened. While they talked and questioned together, Jesus himself came near, and went with them. But their eyes were kept from recognizing him. He said to them, "What are you talking about as you walk, and are sad?" One of them, named Cleopas, answered him, "Are you the only stranger in Jerusalem who doesn't know the things which have happened there in these days?" He said to them, "What things?" They said to him, "The things concerning Jesus, the Nazarene, who was a prophet mighty in deed and word before God and all the people; and how the chief priests and our rulers delivered him up to be condemned to death, and crucified him. But we were hoping that it was he who would redeem Israel. Yes, and besides all this, it is now the third day since these things happened. Also, certain women of our company amazed us, having arrived early at the tomb; and when they didn't find his body, they came saying that they had also seen a vision of angels, who said that he was alive. Some of us went to the tomb, and found it just like the women had said, but they didn't see him."

He said to them, "Foolish men, and slow of heart to believe in all that the prophets have spoken! Didn't the Christ have to suffer these things and to enter into his glory?" Beginning from Moses and from all the prophets, he explained to them in all the Scriptures the things concerning himself. They came near to the village where they were going, and he acted like he would go further.

Jesus reveals himself to the two disciples (Lk 24:29)

They urged him, saying, "Stay with us, for it is almost evening, and the day is almost over." He went in to stay with them. When he had sat down at the table with them, he took the bread and gave thanks. Breaking it, he gave it to them. Their eyes were opened and they recognized him, then he vanished out of their sight. They said to one another, "Weren't our hearts burning within us, while he spoke to us along the way, and while he opened the Scriptures to us?" They rose up that very hour, returned to Jerusalem, and found the eleven gathered together, and those who were with them, saying, "The Lord is risen indeed, and has appeared to Simon!"

They return to Jerusalem to warn (Lk 24:33)

They rose up that very hour, returned to Jerusalem, and found the eleven gathered together, and those who were with them, saying, "The Lord is risen indeed, and has appeared to Simon!"

Jesus appears to the disciples without Thomas (Lk 24:35)

They related the things that happened along the way, and how he was recognized by them in the breaking of the bread. As they said these things, Jesus himself stood among them, and said to them, "Peace be to you." But they were terrified and filled with fear, and supposed that they had seen a spirit.

He said to them, "Why are you troubled? Why do doubts arise in your hearts? See my hands and my feet, that it is truly me. Touch me and see, for a spirit doesn't have flesh and bones, as you see that I have." When he had said this, he showed them his hands and his feet. While they still didn't believe for joy, and wondered, he said to them, "Do you have anything here to eat?"

They gave him a piece of a broiled fish and some honeycomb. He took them, and ate in front of them. He said to them, "This is what I told you, while I was still with you, that all things which are written in the law of Moses, the prophets, and the psalms, concerning me must be fulfilled." Then he opened their minds, that they might understand the Scriptures.

Apostles receive the Holy Spirit *(Jn 20:21)*

Jesus therefore said to them again, "Peace be to you. As the Father has sent me, even so I send you." When he had said this, he breathed on them, and said to them, "Receive the Holy Spirit! If you forgive anyone's sins, they have been forgiven them. If you retain anyone's sins, they have been retained."

Thomas' unbelief *(Jn 20:24)*

But Thomas, one of the twelve, called Didymus, wasn't with them when Jesus came. The other disciples therefore said to him, "We have seen the Lord!" But he said to them, "Unless I see in his hands the print of the nails, put my finger into the print of the nails, and put my hand into his side, I will not believe."

Jesus appears to Thomas *(Jn 20:26)*

After eight days again his disciples were inside and Thomas was with them. Jesus came, the doors being locked, and stood in the middle, and said, "Peace be to you." Then he said to Thomas,

"Reach here your finger, and see my hands. Reach here your hand, and put it into my side. Don't be unbelieving, but believing." Thomas answered him, "My Lord and my God!" Jesus said to him, "Because you have seen me, you have believed. Blessed are those who have not seen, and have believed."

He appears to seven disciples (Second miraculous catch - Jn 21:1)

After these things, Jesus revealed himself again to the disciples at the sea of Tiberias. He revealed himself this way. Simon Peter, Thomas called Didymus, Nathanael of Cana in Galilee, and the sons of Zebedee, and two others of his disciples were together. Simon Peter said to them, "I'm going fishing." They told him, "We are also coming with you." They immediately went out, and entered into the boat.

That night, they caught nothing. But when day had already come, Jesus stood on the beach, yet the disciples didn't know that it was Jesus. Jesus therefore said to them, "Children, have you anything to eat?" They answered him, "No." He said to them, "Cast the net on the right side of the boat, and you will find some." They cast it therefore, and now they weren't able to draw it in for the multitude of fish.

That disciple therefore whom Jesus loved said to Peter, "It's the Lord!" So, when Simon Peter heard that it was the Lord, he wrapped his coat around himself (for he was naked), and threw himself into the sea. But the other disciples came in the little boat (for they were not far from the land, but about two hundred cubits away), dragging the net full of fish. So, when they got out on the land, they saw a fire of coals there, with fish and bread laid on it.

Jesus said to them, "Bring some of the fish which you have just caught." Simon Peter went up, and drew the net to land, full of one hundred fifty-three great fish. Even though there were so many, the net wasn't torn. Jesus said to them, "Come and eat breakfast!" None of the disciples dared inquire of him, "Who are you?" knowing that it was the Lord. Then Jesus came and took the bread, gave it to them, and the fish likewise. This is now the third time that Jesus was revealed to his disciples after he had risen from the dead.

Appears to eleven in Galilee *(Mt 28:16)*

But the eleven disciples went into Galilee, to the mountain where Jesus had sent them. When they saw him, they bowed down to him; but some doubted. Jesus came to them and spoke to them, saying, "All authority has been given to me in heaven and on earth.

Appears to over five hundred people *(I Co 15:6)*

Then he appeared to over five hundred brothers at once, most of whom remain until now, but some have also fallen asleep.

The great commission *(Mt 28:19, Mk 16:16)*

Go and make disciples of all nations, baptizing them in the name of the Father and of the Son and of the Holy Spirit, teaching them to observe all things that I commanded you. Behold, I am with you always, even to the end of the age." Amen. He who believes and is baptized will be saved; but he who disbelieves will be condemned.

The signs will follow those who believe *(Mk 16:17)*

These signs will accompany those who believe: in my name they will cast out demons; they will speak with new languages; they will take up serpents; and if they drink any deadly thing, it will in no way hurt them; they will lay hands on the sick, and they will recover."

Jesus opens the disciples' understanding *(Lk 24:44)*

He said to them, "This is what I told you, while I was still with you, that all things which are written in the law of Moses, the prophets, and the psalms, concerning me must be fulfilled." Then he opened their minds, that they might understand the Scriptures.

He said to them, "Thus it is written, and thus it was necessary for the Christ to suffer and to rise from the dead the third day, and that repentance and remission of sins should be preached in his name to all the nations, beginning at Jerusalem. You are witnesses of these things.

The last instructions (Lk 24:49, Ac 1:4)

Behold, I send out the promise of my Father on you. But wait in the city of Jerusalem until you are clothed with power from on high." He led them out as far as Bethany, and he lifted up his hands, and blessed them. Being assembled together with them, he commanded them, "Don't depart from Jerusalem, but wait for the promise of the Father, which you heard from me. For John indeed baptized in water, but you will be baptized in the Holy Spirit not many days from now."

Therefore, when they had come together, they asked him, "Lord, are you now restoring the kingdom to Israel?" He said to them, "It isn't for you to know times or seasons which the Father has set within his own authority. But you will receive power when the Holy Spirit has come upon you. You will be witnesses to me in Jerusalem, in all Judea and Samaria, and to the uttermost parts of the earth."

The ascension of the Lord (Lk 24:50, Ac 1:10)

He led them out as far as Bethany, and he lifted up his hands, and blessed them. While he blessed them, he withdrew from them, and was carried up into heaven. While they were looking steadfastly into the sky as he went, behold, two men stood by them in white clothing, who also said, "You men of Galilee, why do you stand looking into the sky? This Jesus, who was received up from you into the sky, will come back in the same way as you saw him going into the sky."

The resurrection of Jesus was the most important event in the history of humanity, not only of Christianity, because He was the only human being to conquer death by His own power and ascend to heaven. Through the resurrection, Jesus proved indisputably to His followers and to the world that everything He preached and promised was true. Those who witnessed this event recognized, once and for all, that Jesus was the Messiah, the Son of God, and that through Him all the prophecies were fulfilled.

Every time Jesus spoke about His death and resurrection, it was as if a veil covered the eyes of His disciples. They heard, but did not understand. All of that changed when they saw the risen Jesus. The fact that He kept the scars of the crucifixion, ate with them, allowed Himself to be touched, and at the same time could pass through closed doors and suddenly disappear, gave them a glimpse of what a glorified body can do. The final demonstration of this body occurred when Jesus ascended to heaven, showing that even the earth had no power to restrain Him.

All this display of glory caused the disciples to follow their calling even to death. There was no return to fishing nor sorrow over being separated from the Master. The disciples endured terrible persecutions and deaths for being witnesses of this Gospel. The experience they had with Jesus during the forty days after the Resurrection further solidified their faith and propelled the spread of the gospel. Thanks to these disciples, the message crossed generations until it reached us. After seeing the risen Jesus, not even death made them deny their faith.

What is the difference between the resurrection of Lazarus and that of Jesus? Lazarus died because of the curse of human sin and later died again. Jesus, on the other hand, without sin, took upon Himself the sins of humanity to redeem it. When He rose again, He was united with His glorified body and never experienced death again, but eternal life at the Father's side.

The Benefits of Jesus' Resurrection

The resurrection of Jesus granted us many benefits, such as: the right to future resurrection, eternal life, justification before the Father, authority over the powers of evil, victory over death, new life, and the Holy Spirit dwelling in us.

Future Resurrection

"For if we believe that Jesus died and rose again, even so God will bring with Him those who sleep in Jesus." 1 Thessalonians 4:14

Eternal Life for All Who Believe

"I am the resurrection and the life. He who believes in Me, though he may die, he shall live." John 11:25

Justified by His Resurrection

Jesus presented His sacrifice for humanity to the Father, and because He rose again, it means that the Father accepted His sacrifice and we were raised together with Him. For this reason, we are also seated with Jesus on His throne.

Through the sacrifice, the blood, and the resurrection of Jesus, God receives us as if we had never sinned. We were saved by His blood and restored by His resurrection!

Victory Over Death and Principalities

Jesus achieved victory over death and the evil principalities through the Resurrection. "I am He who lives, and was dead, and behold, I am alive forevermore, and I have the keys of Hades and of Death." Revelation 1:18

By conquering death, Jesus secured justification and new life for those who believe. "Through His resurrection, we are declared righteous before God, for Christ overcame sin and reconciled us with the Father." Romans 4:25

New Life

New life was granted to us through His resurrection, as we read in 1 Peter 1:3: "Blessed be the God and Father of our Lord Jesus Christ, who according to His abundant mercy has begotten us again to a living hope through the resurrection of Jesus Christ from the dead."

Temple of the Holy Spirit

After the resurrection, Jesus promised the Holy Spirit as the Comforter. "I will pray the Father, and He will give you another Helper, that He may abide with you forever—the Spirit of truth, whom the world cannot receive, because it neither sees Him nor knows Him; but you know Him, for He dwells with you and will be in you." John 14:16-17

The religious leaders did not understand how Jesus would destroy the temple and rebuild it in three days. They had no idea He was referring to His own body, and that through His resurrection, humanity would become the new temple of God's Holy Spirit, as stated in 1 Corinthians 6:19-20: "Or do you not know that your body is the temple of the Holy Spirit who is in you, whom you have from God, and you are not your own? For you were bought at a price; therefore glorify God in your body and in your spirit, which are God's."

All of this was only possible because Jesus faced and defeated death, hell, and the powers of evil through the authority of His Word and the power given to Him by God. The Father testified to Him, and His word was the same as God's.

If Jesus had not risen, our faith would be in vain, because death would have ended His promises and His ministry. However, death could not hold Him—hell lost its keys! All the powers of evil were disarmed, publicly humiliated, and defeated forever by the cross. He is risen!

What stood out to you the most?

_____

_____

_____

_____

_____

How can this reflection enhance your spiritual life?

_____

_____

_____

_____

What would you say to Jesus today?

_____

_____

_____

_____

"Blessed be the God and Father of our Lord Jesus Christ. According to His great mercy, He has caused us to be born again to a living hope through the resurrection of Jesus Christ from the dead. And the result of this is an inheritance that is imperishable, undefiled, and unfading."
1 Peter 1:3-4

www.ingramcontent.com/pod-product-compliance
Lightning Source LLC
Chambersburg PA
CBHW032118040426

42449CB00005B/185